Birth of a Church

Birth of a Church

Joseph Nangle, OFM

ORBIS BOOKS

Maryknoll, New York 10545

Founded in 1970, Orbis Books endeavors to publish works that enlighten the mind, nourish the spirit, and challenge the conscience. The publishing arm of the Maryknoll Fathers and Brothers, Orbis seeks to explore the global dimensions of the Christian faith and mission, to invite dialogue with diverse cultures and religious traditions, and to serve the cause of reconciliation and peace. The books published reflect the views of their authors and do not represent the official position of the Maryknoll Society. To learn more about Maryknoll and Orbis Books, please visit our website at www.maryknoll.org.

Manufactured in the United States of America
ISBN

Library of Congress Cataloging-in-Publication Data

Nangle, Joseph.
  Birth of a church / Joseph Nangle.
    p. cm.
  ISBN 1-57075-560-4 (pbk.)
  1. Most Holy Name Parish (Lima, Peru)—History—20th century.
2. Lima (Peru)—Church history—20th century.   3. Liberation
theology—Lima—Peru. 4. Nangle, Joseph. I. Title.
  BX4624.L5N36   2004
  282'.8525—dc22
                        2004006508

*To my Franciscan province of the Most Holy Name,
in heartfelt gratitude for the opportunity to serve the church
and people of Bolivia and Peru.*

Contents

Acknowledgements

Every book has a thousand parents, and that is especially true in the present case. Every page of this book underscores the obvious fact that the experience recounted here was lived by the members of Most Holy Name Parish in Lima, Peru. So, in the very first place, my lasting gratitude to all of those parishioners.

Margaret Schellenberg and Marie Dennis first listened to this story and validated it for me as I struggled to make sense of it upon returning permanently to the United States. Those Monday evening sessions in their kitchens, conversing about what I had experienced at the parish in Lima, made me think that the story might have relevance for North America. I shall always be grateful for those conversations, which also proved to be therapeutic for me. It seemed only fitting that I would ask my dear friend Marie Dennis to write a foreword to this book, since from those early days she has observed closely and affirmed my efforts to live the experience of Most Holy Name Parish back here in the United States.

The late Phillip Scharper, founding editor of Orbis Books, first encouraged me to write this book. I might never have had the courage to put it all on paper had it not been for his professional opinion that my story had merit. Mr. Scharper's successor at Orbis, Robert Ellsberg, stuck with me when the book was in its awkward infancy and adolescence, and he saw its potential for making a difference in the North American church when I finished writing. To these two remarkable men, also, my heartfelt thanks.

Janet Mock, SSJ, Executive Director of the Religious Formation Conference, and Mary Ann Buckley, SHCJ, read the manuscript as outsiders to the story, and generously vouched for its usefulness to the church in the United States. Scott Wright and Jean Stoken of my home Assisi Community took the time to offer editing and stylistic commentaries; Sister Dianna Ortiz and the other members of that community never failed in their encouragement along the way; Co-Director Megeen White and the staff at Franciscan Mission Service generously gave me time off to work on the book.

My Franciscan brother, George Corrigan, generously provided computer expertise and all-round encouragement so that I could write this story. And Orbis Books provided a perceptive copyeditor, Ellen Calmus, who spotted and corrected faulty syntax throughout the book.

Finally, I must acknowledge a life-long debt of gratitude to theologian Father Gustavo Gutiérrez and all of the priests, religious and laity of Latin America who accepted us North Americans in their midst, educated us to their unique world and sent us back as missioners to our home country. May that wonderful history one day be written.

Foreword

From the outside it was a seamless transition. In 1975 Joseph Nangle, OFM, returned to the United States after 15 years in Latin America, bringing with him the story you are about to read—a collage of experiences and relationships to which he has held himself accountable for thirty years. His return was personally difficult, signaling the end of an extremely important era in his life, but it was clear to those who met him in the U.S. that while his heart had never left Lima, the next step in his mission for social justice was appropriately here.

Within weeks of Joe's renewed encounter with the U.S. church, he was unpacking the treasure he had in his soul to explore its relevance in this world. He was convinced of the connection between the affluence and power of a few people, whether they lived in Peru or in the United States, and the terrible poverty and exclusion of so many he had come to love in Lima. He began to apply here the lessons he had learned and insights he had gathered there, and to nurture carefully any inkling that he encountered about how to do justice on this new phase of his journey.

St. Luke's in McLean, Virginia, my parish at that time, was an early beneficiary of Joe's unwavering belief in the powerful witness to justice that was born at Most Holy Name in Lima, the parish that is the subject of this book. As an upper-middle-class parish quite similar to Most Holy Name, we were particularly receptive to his message. We were already trying to understand what a parish commitment to social justice might entail and had taken some steps on our own—exploring the relationship of justice to charity, challenging the affluent lifestyles enjoyed by most parishioners that contrasted painfully with poverty in our own county and in nearby Washington, D.C., and educating ourselves about some of the important social justice issues in the metropolitan area. We were also concerned about certain aspects of U.S. foreign policy and had begun to hear about Medellín and the newly articulated commitment to the poor of the Latin American church. I clearly remember reading books by Paulo Freire and Gustavo Gutiérrez, but their context was too far from my own for me to have any real sense of their message.

In early 1975 our parish council agreed to allow the Community Concerns Committee, of which I was then chair, to hire a staff person part time. We carefully crafted a job description. We were looking for someone to work part time in our suburban parish to help with "education to justice, lifestyle change and action." By some miracle or movement of the Spirit, a friend gave Joe a copy of our job announcement and he applied. In retrospect, it was a perfect match.

Shortly after he began to work with us, a dear friend and insightful colleague, Margaret Schellenberg, suggested that we ask him to tell us his story. Every Monday night, week after week during the fall of 1975, the three of us gathered. Margaret and I listened to his experiences in mission—first, his mission in Bolivia, where he encountered extreme poverty, honed his language skills and ministered to people marginalized by their own society and the world—and later in Peru, where his own conversion was occasioned by a church that had made a preferential option for the poor, and especially by his impoverished friends like Olga and José, who bore daily the brutal insults wealth can inflict on the poor. First, Margaret and I, then our parish, and later thousands of U.S. Americans came to know José and Olga Valencia and so many others who graced Joe's path in Latin America—and to understand the reign of God as intrinsically related to their pursuit of liberation, of social justice and peace. Theirs is the story you will read in the pages that follow. We heard it as a powerful invitation to continue the journey we had already begun.

Joe's job in the parish was part time, but his presence brought us face to face with another world. His Franciscan commitment to pastoral ministry as an essential component of prophetic leadership helped move our parish, set as it was in the wealthy, almost entirely white suburbia of the time, as far as it could then go toward a more just way of being community in a broken world. His rich experience in Bolivia and Peru helped us understand better the powerful movement toward liberation in the Latin American church and interpret what kind of response to this movement we ought to be making as middle-class Catholic Christians in the United States.

We inched along in our parish. In many ways, our efforts to shape a justice agenda were probably too ambitious and lacking in pedagogical or organizing skills. Unlike Most Holy Name Parish in Lima, we did not have the involvement of the pastor or the unwavering support of the parish council. I think we failed more often than we succeeded in engaging the majority of parishioners. But the fact that we as a parish did try to read the gospel in our own context and to ask hard questions about its application to our communal and personal lives was most important.

Though worlds apart, the two parishes faced a number of very similar challenges. In Joe's first year at St. Luke's, as part of a broader evaluation of our parochial school, we presented a case for expanding the educational mission of the parish to the poor by closing St. Luke's School. Since the public schools in our county were some of the finest in the nation, our committee proposed that we instead support a nearby inner city parochial school that could serve as an alternative to the then-seriously-deficient public schools in the District of Columbia. St. Luke's School stayed open, but important questions about social justice were at least on the table.

Also in those years, a decision had to be made about whether or not to build a new church that would cost millions of dollars. A very thorough public discernment process preceded the final decision; as part of the process, serious consideration was given to issues of social justice. I was devastated when the decision was made to go ahead with an expensive building program, but, again, concerns for social justice were at least discussed.

As 1976 and the U.S. bicentennial celebration approached, we participated in the excellent process called "Liberty and Justice for All," designed by the Center of Concern for the U.S. Catholic Conference. Small groups all over the parish, including among those not previously "warm" to the work of our committee, reflected on assigned themes—humankind, nationhood, church, personhood, and so on—in preparation for the original Call to Action meeting planned to be held in Detroit. Many of us hoped that the Call to Action would be the Medellín of the U.S. church and were subsequently left bitterly disappointed when the powerful and prophetic documents it produced were never adequately promulgated.

In some ways that process was a high point of the work we did for social justice in the McLean Parish. A new diocese created in Northern Virginia changed our area's focus somewhat, and thereafter the parish ground seemed less fertile, less open, less willing to participate in the work for social transformation.

What seems evident thirty years later, however, is how fertile that ground was and how profoundly affected were the hearts and minds of people in our McLean, Virginia, parish and beyond. Many have visibly integrated a commitment to social justice into their work and their lives—encouraged not only by the efforts we made in the parish to educate or challenge or reshape our lives, but especially by the presence and life experience of people like Joe Nangle. He gently, persistently, moved about in that parish and beyond—to communities all over the Washington metropolitan area—in fact, all over the U.S.—inviting people into his stories and living in a way that made a prophetic message for middle-class U.S. Americans credible and palatable.

The encounter of St. Luke's Parish in McLean, Virginia, with the parish of Most Holy Name in Lima, Peru, was very significant for our middle-class U.S. community. Though we never had a sister parish relationship, I believe that if we had we would have understood each other's successes and each other's failures. Our reality in McLean was cushioned in many ways from the impoverished world of Most Holy Name, and our efforts were small compared to theirs, but their struggle to make real an option for the poor made great sense to us, and we found their example most encouraging.

Now that the world is more tightly integrated, we know well that the harsh reality of Lima's barrios that Joe observed in the late 1960s and early 1970s continues to dehumanize and destroy—and that the root causes are related to U.S. lifestyles and to economic and political decisions made here.

The story of Most Holy Name Parish is a challenging example of maturing Christians attempting to implement the gospel vision of social justice in their own community of faith. It is an amazing gift—most relevant to the vocation of U.S. parishes in the context of a world still divided by violence and poverty, yet yearning for justice and peace.

Marie Dennis

Introduction

About four o'clock on a hot Saturday afternoon I answered the phone in the friary and heard an excited voice on the line pleading with me to come out to the nearby Pan American highway. A little boy had been run over and killed by a hit-and-run driver and bystanders thought they recognized the victim as one of our parochial school children; his body was lying on the side of that busy roadway; could I please hurry over and take charge.

Two of the sisters who staffed the parish school drove with me the short distance to the accident site. We parked on the side of the highway and quickly walked over to the little form lying just off the pavement. Sadly, we confirmed the fact that the dead child was indeed one of our students, nine-year-old José Valencia, the eldest child of an extremely poor family. I recall thinking as I looked down at José's face that he seemed to wear a kind of resigned expression, as if he had known that his life could end this way. It was, I thought afterward, pretty much the way I had remembered him in life. Poor kids like José often struck me as passive, almost indolent, probably due to their chronic undernourishment and the low energy levels it causes.

In fact it was his family's ongoing struggle to feed themselves which had brought José on that summer afternoon to the spot where he would meet his fate. As he did three or four times every week, the youngster had set out earlier to beg scraps of food left over from the midday meals of the upper-middle-class families in the area. What he managed to collect at the doorways of the spacious homes in that affluent suburb became the evening meal for his parents and siblings. As a nine-year old, José already had major responsibilities for his family's survival.

On that fateful afternoon, we conjectured that he must have gotten distracted as he walked along the shoulder of the Pan America Highway on his way home. Perhaps he was playing kick-the-can or throwing stones or doing any number of things a young boy would do on a summer afternoon. Whatever the reason, he seemed to have wandered a little too far onto the highway and, according to the eye-witnesses, was run over by a pickup truck, which immediately sped away. The little cooking pot, which José used to collect the leftover food, lay crushed on the highway, its pathetic contents strewn around as birds swooped in to pick at them.

We placed newspapers over José's face and body to protect him from flies and bugs, then the sisters and I led the folks who had gathered in a prayer over the dead child. We learned that the police had been notified of the accident and figured it would be just a short wait for permission to remove José. What we didn't know right away was that for the police the boy's name and address marked him as Indian and therefore poor, so that on a Saturday in summertime the investigation of the accident would move with agonizing slowness.

As the quarter hours turned into hours and night drew on, our frustration mounted. We continued to stand by the side of the road next to José's small form, praying, talking about the tragedy before us, phoning repeatedly for police assistance—and waiting. Their inaction seemed to express a blatant indifference to this child's death and the need for a decent disposal of his body, but the anger that welled up in us had no where to go. Expressing it to the authorities, we knew, would only slow things down even more.

Meanwhile, José's mother, Olga, noticed that the time for his arrival home had long since come and gone, so she boarded a local bus which covered the route he normally took. As the bus approached the spot where we were standing on the opposite side of the highway, Olga saw our little group clustered around the form with its telltale covering of newspapers. She recognized her son's cotton jeans protruding from underneath and she screamed for the bus driver to let her off. But he refused, insisting that she had to wait until the next regular bus stop, about a quarter of a mile further up the road. When she was finally able to get off at the stop, she crossed the highway and came running frantically toward us, crying out her son's name again and again.

We embraced Olga, cried with her as she looked down on her

dead son's face and battered body, prayed a little with her and did our best to speak some words of consolation. Those gestures all felt so hollow and inadequate. We knew that she had lost her oldest child, a boy who had begun to help her and the family as they eked out a life for themselves. We felt entirely helpless to console her and I remember wondering where God was in Olga's tragedy.[1]

Our little group stood there until about 8:30 or 9:00 that sultry February evening, when, finally, a police cruiser pulled up alongside us and an indifferent voice from inside the car told us that we could take the body away. However, the voice said, we would have to bring José to the city morgue. The criminal circumstances of his death, a hit-and-run accident, required further investigation, including an autopsy. So Olga held her son's limp body in her lap as the sisters and I drove in silence to the city "morgue"—a large room with open windows in the basement of Lima's general hospital. We carried the body in and laid it on one of the concrete slabs alongside several other corpses, then took Olga home.

Early the next morning José's parents came knocking at the friary door and asked me to go with them to the local jail where the driver of the pickup truck was in custody, charged with aggravated manslaughter. Either he had been tracked down and arrested or else he had turned himself in when he sobered up and realized what had happened the day before. The Valencias knew that someone with a pickup truck should have a way to pay the $75 it would take to give their boy the sort of decent funeral they could never afford. They felt my presence with them would give them some leverage in their demands, and I was more than willing to help them. So José's parents and I spent that Sunday seated in the cellblock making repeated and, in the end, futile attempts to negotiate the price of their son's burial with the man responsible for his death. The accused driver, having his own legal problems to deal with, was not willing to settle out of court with José's parents. He absolutely would not budge and I remember thinking as we saw the impasse grow that Olga and her husband, like so many of their kind, didn't even have the luxury of mourning their little boy.

On Sunday afternoon I drove alone to the morgue to see if the autopsy had been completed and found the doctors in no hurry to examine José's body and sign the all-important death certificate. They said it was Sunday, after all, and that they were very busy—once again the unspoken attitude that since the boy was from a poor family, his case could wait. I was experiencing exactly what poor people always hear: come back later. It was frustrating and enraging.

After a long wait at the morgue, around noon on Monday Olga and I finally obtained the death certificate and release of José's body. We went to a carpenter's shop near the morgue and purchased the cheapest coffin we could find. We placed José's remains in the box, then drove to the Valencias' home for the traditional viewing and funeral. José's mother and father still had no idea how they were going to pay for the boy's burial.

The house, like all the others in their slum neighborhood, was a miserable affair. It consisted of one room with a dirt floor, the walls made of straw matting and the roof of flattened cardboard boxes tied to the matting at the four corners. Beds lined two sides of the room and on the opposite side from the beds were the kerosene stove, cooking utensils and the little table where the family took their meals. Practically the entire life of the Valencia family took place in this hovel. An emaciated dog, a few chickens and several guinea pigs, raised for an occasional "special" meal, scurried underfoot, while José's younger brothers and sisters played in and around the doorway, their dirty faces and clothes testifying to the serious water shortage in the area.

These little ones gaped at us as we carried the box containing their brother's body into the center of the room and set it on a table for the all-night viewing. Neighbors of the Valencias, all living in the same economic and social circumstances, began to gather late that Monday afternoon for the vigil. They were genuinely sympathetic to Olga and her husband, knowing only too well from their own experience what the death of a growing boy meant to families like theirs.

Meanwhile, the cost of the burial arrangements continued to be a pressing concern. We approached the local undertaker to ask if he would extend credit to the Valencias (backed by my promise of payment) so that they could carry out a traditional and dignified funeral for their son. However, the man absolutely refused to make any funeral arrangements unless the family prepaid in full. As a struggling, poor person himself, he was afraid that if he went ahead with the burial, relying on their word, the Valencias would forget about their promise once the funeral was over. He said that for him it would be just one more uncollected bill.

As Monday night gave way to Tuesday morning and the end of the all-night viewing approached, both the social and practical urgent need to bury José became the major preoccupation for his parents and me. To hold the body longer would demonstrate to the whole neighborhood that the Valencias did not even have enough money to take care of this basic and final act of love and respect for their son, which would be a terrible embarrassment for them. On a practical level, José's unembalmed body, having lain around now nearly three full days in the summer heat, was showing signs of discoloration. Something had to be done.

As the neighbors took their leave for home and work early on Tuesday, I approached José's father and mother and told them that we had no choice but to bury the boy ourselves. They knew what that meant. We would take the body to the local cemetery, rent a niche (burials take place above ground in Lima) in the poor people's section reserved for just such cases and lay José to rest. No undertaker, no cortege, no ceremony. The Valencias understood, too, that doing the burial this way meant that after a week or two the rented niche would be cleared out for another indigent person and José would be interred unceremoniously in a common grave—a large pit in the ground.

But at this point José's mother and father had no choice and they reluctantly agreed with my "solution." The three of us took the coffin out to the car, drove to the cemetery, where we rented a grave, carried José to the assigned niche and placed the little coffin inside. We stood for a time at the temporary gravesite, Olga weeping quietly. I led our sad little group of three in some of the official burial prayers on behalf of José's eternal rest and happiness. We shared some thoughts about his life and the circumstances of his death, then turned away and drove back in silence to their house. I stayed with them for a while, sitting on one of the beds making small talk and assuring them that we would be more than happy to celebrate the customary Mass on the eighth day after the boy's death. Then I left them to take up the threads of their desperate lives—now without José.

A Metaphor

The tragic death of José Valencia and the equally tragic story of his parents' struggle to get him buried stand as a defining metaphor for the religious and lay people who engaged in the founding and early years of Most Holy Name Parish in Lima, Peru. It was a parish situated in a wealthy, suburban enclave of that city, surrounded by an ocean of people like the Valencias. We founded the parish with a particular awareness of and attention to its attractive, influential, privileged middle-class families and gradually came to respond to the poor, underprivileged and dispossessed human beings in our midst. We also became increasingly aware of the relationship between those two cultures which made up Most Holy Name—the wealthy and the poor, the haves and the have-nots—and how they interacted, or failed to interact, with one another.

For me, José's and his family's story has come to stand as a defining metaphor for all Christian ministry. The entire world is made up of relatively small wealthy sectors surrounded by a sea of poverty, oppression and exclusion. What I experienced during the eleven years I spent as the first pastor of Most Holy Name Parish has continued to disturb and challenge me in the many areas of religious work in which I have engaged and in my observation of the work of others.

At Most Holy Name we learned that the Valencias' story was not an isolated event, some terrible but marginal occurrence easily passed over as an exception to most people's experience in this world. Rather, the Valencias represented the norm in Peru, the way most people live there. In fact, the way they lived was the way a growing majority of human beings across the globe have lived and continue to live today.

We who founded Most Holy Name Parish came to understand that the tragic story of José's life and death and burial and millions of similar stories can be traced to understandable and measurable societal realities: inequitable economic opportunities, lack of education, subhuman housing, hunger, joblessness, racism, classism, sexism—and bad theology. José was not the victim of bad luck or poor judgment on his parents' part or, God help us, some serious flaw in his family genes. The Valencias were decent people who begged only to be allowed the opportunity to provide for the basic needs of their family. I had come to know Olga slightly in the years before her son's death, and her constant plea to me and to anyone who would listen was for work—any kind of work—so that she could augment the pathetic income her husband was barely able to earn. The way places like Peru and Latin America and most of the world are organized produces millions and millions of Valencias. This is what we learned, and it is a reality that continues to challenge our lives and ministries.

Holy Name Parish was founded just before the Latin American Catholic Church came to a historic consciousness of its obligations toward these impoverished populations. When that consciousness dawned, all of us engaged in the ministry of that parish found ourselves swept up in our church's call for personal and institutional conversion. That call was so compelling. Living and working in the world of the privileged few and the numberless José Valencias who constituted Most Holy Name Parish made our decision to join the Latin-American/Peruvian church in making "a preferential option for the poor" what some people call a "no-brainer" for the pastoral ministers, both lay and religious, at Most Holy Name. We simply could not do otherwise. That is the dramatic story of this book: how we who were serving a middle- and upper-middle-class parish experienced and integrated into every aspect of our own lives and the life of that parish the lessons learned from people like the Valencias, interpreted and mediated by the social teaching of the institutional church there.

In many ways the story of Most Holy Name Parish is an improbable one which, I believe, makes it all the more relevant and challenging for other faith communities. Why and how did this comfortable and popular parish turn itself around—be converted—and move from its place of privilege to the risky side of the poor? One would not have expected it from such an affluent "successful" parish, nor particularly from the religious to whom it was entrusted: priests and lay brothers and sisters from the United States. For we began the parish with little or no understanding of the social forces at work in Latin America; we came to the new assignment quite innocent of the social imperatives of Jesus' message. In the end it was the poor who converted the church; they converted the parish; and they converted us.

What is more, the story of Most Holy Name Parish during the 1960s and 1970s in suburban Lima, Peru, cannot be circumscribed by that time and that place. I believe it has a projection that questions and challenges every place where the gospel of Jesus Christ is preached and acted on. It is the story of every parish, *especially* those parishes located in our own affluent First World.

To me it is abundantly clear now that the lessons learned from the institutional conversion of Most Holy Name and its ministers apply especially to parish life in the United States. Through the experience of a decade as pastor of this suburban parish in Lima, Peru, I learned that no Christian organization—be it diocese or parish, religious congregation, parochial or diocesan school, Bible group or intentional community, or the people who belong to them—exists for itself. The church at every level of her life and in every one of her members is there on behalf of and in service to God's Reign of universal dignity and justice, called to announce joyfully all that heralds the coming of that Reign and to denounce clearly what stands in its way. I came away from my eleven years as pastor of Most Holy Name with the deepest possible conviction that to make anything less of church institutions is to betray the gospel message for which those institutions exist in the first place. After my return to this country I found that too often our U.S. churches err by neglecting or ignoring this prophetic mandate and become unexamined, unchallenging comfort zones for their members. The lessons I learned at Most Holy Name taught me that this is the antithesis of what the gospel calls for and has become a scandal in our time. In addition this failure runs the risk of making the church in this First World increasingly irrelevant. People will not take a church seriously that does not come to grips with the real world of suffering, injustice, wars and ecological devastation.

My entire purpose, therefore, in attempting to tell this story is a hope that it will serve as both a challenge and an encouragement for making all our Christian institutions and the people who belong to them as prophetic as they are pastoral. My experience in Peru brought me to the conviction that such a gospel mandate is not only necessary but absolutely doable. It just takes vision and fortitude, gifts of the Spirit.

Notes

[1]This theological and ultimate human question will receive extensive attention throughout this narrative.

CHAPTER 1

A Parish Is Born

It began with a traditional Sunday Eucharist on a sun-drenched summer morning in February of 1964. As the newly appointed founding pastor of Most Holy Name Parish in a newly developed suburb of Lima, Peru, I celebrated the Mass on a makeshift altar in an open field where a year later the parish house would stand. I remember the glare of the sun in my eyes during the liturgy and how much I had to squint in order to focus on the book and the altar vessels placed on the white linen cloths.

During the month or so since my arrival in Peru I had driven around and left written announcements about the inaugural Mass in most of the few dozen homes that comprised the new parish, so that about thirty or forty people showed up at the appointed hour. In typically Peruvian style they were very cordial, and of course they were curious about the new parish and its priest.

That first Mass was pre-Vatican II in every sense. We would hardly recognize it today. I recited the ancient Latin prayers of the Roman rite standing with my back to the congregation, and using the stylized, formal gestures of the Mass which were so familiar to all of us in those days, and entirely obsolete just a couple of years later. Indeed, everything about the gathering spoke of church life as it had been for centuries, with the priest as the central actor of the Mass and the people as bystanders. I preached a sermon centered on the Eucharist and the other sacraments in which I invited the parishioners to unite with me as I led them in building the parochial community. I conveyed a strong and comfortable sense of my call to lead the new parish, something which was no doubt accepted by everyone present. In

1

those days no one would think of questioning or objecting to those sorts of words because that's the way it was with the church. I would be in charge, hopefully in a friendly and inviting way; the people needed simply to help out wherever they could. All very neat and traditional, all on the verge of collapse.

By early 1964 the Second Vatican Council was at its halfway point with two sessions still to come. We were only beginning to feel the profound changes, which the Council would bring to every level of church life. In the minds of our little group gathered there that February morning, there was not the slightest inkling of the Latin Americanization that would soon sweep across the Peruvian church and radically challenge our understanding of God, faith and church. The great Medellín Conference, which four years later would prophetically apply the teachings of Second Vatican Council to the realities of South and Central America, remained a distant dream in the minds of a few visionary church people.

During the sermon and after the service I told the folks that this Mass was the definitive beginning of Most Holy Name and that Sunday Eucharist would be celebrated each week thenceforth. I made no mention of Peru's social realities, of the grinding poverty experienced by most people there, because I didn't know anything about those issues and they didn't occupy much of my thinking. Five years later, given what Most Holy Name Parish would become, this oversight would seem incredible. After the Mass, the people and I stood around for a while and chatted. People complimented me on my facility with the Spanish language and there were wishes for success and promises of help whenever and wherever it might be needed. I asked each one's name and promised to visit their homes before too long. As I drove back to where I was staying, I felt that all in all it had been a successful, if modest, first step. Most Holy Name Parish was on its way.

The Pastor

On that February day in 1964 I was thirty-one years of age, having spent six years a priest, four of them in my Franciscan Order's Bolivian mission. When my superiors informed me that I was being sent to Lima, Peru, to begin a new parish, I told them I thought they were crazy. I was too young, I said, too inexperienced; someone older should be given the assignment. That was what I really thought. But in my heart of hearts I was thrilled to have this opportunity and brash enough to think I could do a credible job of getting this new ministry off the ground.

Something of my own background is relevant here at the beginning of this story and I offer it in the hope that these references do not come across as self-serving or self-centered. But the way in which the new parish began and developed was influenced both positively and negatively by my history and personality. More importantly, the personal and pastoral style of this young, pre-Vatican II priest—me— became a major part of the story I wish to tell in this book. Most Holy Name Parish and I began under one paradigm, one set of rules, one very narrow world view, and in a few years moved to entirely different ones.

As a member of Holy Name Province of the Franciscan Order of Friars Minor with headquarters in New York City, I had studied a theology in the U.S. which we would describe today as conservative, other-worldly, defensive, abstract—the reader can choose the adjective. Human problems had ready-made, one-size-fits-all solutions, with an accompanying spirituality that was tied to each person's relationship with God. Very little of the church's social teaching made its way into our studies, so my generation came to priestly ordination without the benefit of a wider pastoral view other than that of the individual person pretty much in isolation from his or her historical surroundings. It was a "God and me," "God and you" outlook. We did, however, receive excellent Franciscan training and example with regard to the compassion and kindness with which we were expected to treat people in our priestly ministry. And so we emerged from our five or six years of seminary studies as "all-purpose priests," ready and more than willing to take on any ministry we were given, good with people, though quite bound by the rules and regulations of our 1950s church—and totally ahistorical.

During my seminary years I had looked forward to the occasional visits from our Franciscan missioners and felt a stirring within me when one of them told us to nurture any thoughts of a missionary calling which we might feel. Without talking much about it during those years of study, I did just as that missioner had urged. So it wasn't surprising that I volunteered (in the Franciscan Order no one gets sent to an overseas assignment unless he volunteers) for my province's mission in Bolivia shortly after ordination to the priesthood. I was young, athletic, in excellent health, and our Bolivian mission had the reputation of being particularly challenging. Our men who had already gone to Bolivia came back with stories of long treks over rugged terrain, outdoor living, dangerous river crossings or precarious mountain roads and above all ministry to indigenous peoples in remote Andean villages where the priest might show up once or twice each year—just the right stuff to spark the imagination of a twenty-something newly ordained Franciscan. I left New York in January of 1960 full of excitement about the world that awaited me.

Years later a member of my family said that the day I boarded that plane for Latin America marked a break with everything I had known, and he was absolutely right. I would never be the same again. Every missioner experiences it. Some call it "being spoiled for life" in the sense that one's ideas about God and church, about life and what is important, get turned upside down. My experience in this regard underlies much of this story.

For four years I worked in that high Andean country, traveling around by jeep, by mule and on foot, trying to "bring Jesus" to its Indian subsistence farming populations. The experience taught me much about myself—my strengths and weaknesses—because our Franciscan mission in Bolivia at that time was in every sense a "desert experience" for those who volunteered. I came to know how much loneliness I could stand as I worked, often by myself, among people who were vastly different in terms of education and life experience. For example, I don't remember ever seeing an Indigenous woman caress or play with one of her children—perhaps due to embarrassment in the presence of a North American man, or perhaps because of some cultural reticence which I never understood. The contrast with my own culture was profound and often unsettling.

My major assignment in Bolivia took me to a frontier gold-mining town called Caranavi, where nobody cared about religion or spirituality. Making money was the god. Indeed, gold fever there was at such a high pitch that an Italian Franciscan who preceded us Americans in the area had taken one particular gospel mandate quite literally, and shaken the dust of Caranavi from his sandals never to return. Weekend after weekend during those four years I drove by jeep the three or four hours from the mission center where I lived to the Caranavi area. There I celebrated Masses and the other sacraments in three separate locations beginning at 7:00 a.m., often not finishing until 3:00 or 4:00 in the afternoon. (It was rough duty, not helped by the fact that all of us pre-Vatican II priests observed the church's rule of that time, fasting from solid food until the last Eucharist was celebrated.)

My most vivid memory of that raw frontier town of Caranavi was the indifference of the people to my agenda. We operated on different wavelengths—they were exploiting the large deposits of gold in the area; I was trying to build a faith community among them. Arriving there one Sunday morning for the second Mass of the day, I found that the little chapel I had built had been taken over by town officials for local elections. An appeal to those in charge of the voting booths and then to the police got me nowhere (except for a warning by the gendarmes, locked inside their headquarters: "It's not safe out there today, Father").

I spent my first Christmas in Bolivia celebrating Masses in the three pueblos under my care. Three different communities, three Eucharistic celebrations of the Lord's birth—and only one person received Holy Communion. It was unlike anything I had ever experienced in the U.S.

Still, I cannot say that my four years in Bolivia were unhappy. All my brother Franciscans working there were about my age, contemporaries in our studies for the priesthood back in the States and now working together on this Bolivian challenge. Close and lasting friendships were forged among us, precisely because of the goals we shared and the hardships we endured in that rugged country. The mission house where I lived, situated in a place called Coroico on the eastern slopes of the Bolivian Andes, housed seven of us. Every weekend we went out in different directions to the surrounding pueblos and Indian populations, often staying out for days and weeks, doing catechetical and sacramental work. But there were times when several of us would find ourselves back in Coroico at the same time and the sharing and camaraderie we enjoyed are among the happiest memories of my life.

I also had the good fortune to work with women religious during those four years. We spent many hours together in jeeps or on mule back getting from place to place, hours of good conversation and shared impressions from our so very different backgrounds. Most of these women were young members of a Colombian missionary congregation, with wonderful training in the kind of catechetical work we were doing with indigenous Bolivian populations. From my first extended trip with the sisters, I realized that they were really in charge of things: my job was to stay out of their way and be as helpful as I could. Not a bad lesson for a young, North American male cleric. (On that first mission trip with the sisters, one of them asked if she could receive the sacrament of reconciliation, confession. In those days Canon Law forbade any celebration of this sacrament outside of the traditional confessional, and here we were probably one hundred miles from the nearest church. Naturally, the sister and I celebrated the sacrament and I learned a lesson about the applicability of Canon Law in that part of the world. A bishop some years later confirmed that lesson when he said, perhaps only half-jokingly: "Canon Law does not work higher than 5000 feet above sea level.")

It was also thanks to these Colombian sisters that I learned to speak Spanish well. Most of us Americans had gone to Bolivia with barely a smattering of the language, which was an indication of the linguistic and cultural ignorance of so many North Americans who were coming to the Latin American countries in that period. I remember a few weeks after arriving in Bolivia crossing the plaza in Coroico one afternoon accompanied by two young boys. One of them said to the other: "*Este padre, él no sabe nada*" ("This priest, he doesn't know anything"). The youngster of course was referring to the fact that I could hardly say my name in his language. Initial experiences like this got me moving on the language so that I could communicate with the people. I set myself to learning Spanish with an intensity I had rarely brought to other studies before that. In this I had the enormous advantage of regular contact with those women religious from Colombia. When they saw my interest in learning to speak, they made it their business to instruct a willing pupil in the language they were so proud of (it is sometimes said that Colombians speak the best Spanish in Latin America).

In the beginning my struggles with Spanish proved painful, sometimes humiliating and often hilarious. The Colombian sisters insisted from the start that I preach as often as the occasion presented itself, and there were many opportunities for *la charla* (a little talk) during the visits we made to the scores of "pueblos" we had to visit. They would sit near the front of the church or chapel and begin writing down my mistakes almost as soon as I began speaking, a disconcerting experience for this American learner who couldn't help notice the religious in front of him marking down grammatical errors as he was making them. When the sisters couldn't stand it any longer, they would bolt out the door of the chapel, choking with laughter over my stream of malapropisms—laughter which of course I could hear through the open windows as I continued my talk. Then they would return for more. Afterwards the sisters regularly went over the long list of my mistakes, which did not exactly embolden me to try it again at the next pueblo. But time after time these demanding young task-mistresses would insist that I preach. Under that "tough love" I learned the language.

Thus, another lesson I learned in Bolivia was, if not humility, at least the ability not to take myself too seriously. Making mistakes and forever getting corrected pulled me down several pegs on my clerical ladder, and in the end resulted in a good grasp of Spanish and a respect for anyone who tries to learn and use a foreign language. The eventual facility I gained in Spanish, together with all the humiliations I experienced in learning it, stood me in good stead during the rest of my years in Latin America.

I look back on these four years as a difficult, instructive and ultimately happy time, during which I carried on rural ministry among some of the world's poorest and marginalized people. Bolivia is considered the second poorest country in the Western Hemisphere (after Haiti), and at the time I was there it was estimated that barely 11% of the Bolivian people engaged in the economic life of the society—the rest operated on informal barter systems. I came to love the country, but my time there ended abruptly. One afternoon in July of 1963, without any warning, a telegram arrived in Coroico from my Franciscan superiors in the United States naming me as the founding pastor of Most Holy Name Parish in Lima, Peru.

The New York Franciscans had responded to a request from the cardinal of Lima, also a Franciscan, to staff a new parish. They wanted to show support for His Eminence, who was a friend and frequent visitor to our provincial headquarters in New York, and they were also looking for a place of rest and recreation for us Bolivian missioners at a lower altitude (Lima sits on the coast of Peru). For the New York province the parish was a new venture in a country where none of us had worked, and for unknown reasons they chose me for the job. So, without any preparation for the culture I was about to encounter or for the urban ministry among sophisticated Peruvians which awaited me, but with the self-confidence which often goes along with youth and ignorance, I flew alone from La Paz to Lima in the last days of 1963 to begin what would prove to be a great opportunity and a life-changing experience for me.

In those pre-Vatican II days it would never have occurred to me to refuse or even call into question a directive (we called it an "obedi-ence," a direct reference to one of the three vows taken by women and men in religious life) of this sort. In the Franciscan Order, as in all the others, you did what you were told. However, as I mentioned, a short time after my arrival in Peru my New York superiors took the trouble to inquire about my reaction to this new and enormously chal-lenging assignment. I replied that I thought it was a mistake ("crazy" was the word) for them to place so much responsibility on my shoul-ders. After all, I said, I had no experience either in Peru or in a mod-ern Latin American city like Lima; I was exceedingly young for such a responsibility; and I was alone in a new country. Whether it was true or not, the superiors reassured me that everyone connected with the province's leadership had confidence in me and that in fact I would need all of the youthful energy I could muster for the task ahead. In this sense the superiors proved incredibly prescient. For my part, de-spite the misgivings I expressed to the Provincial superior, I jumped into this new assignment right away. For better or worse I possessed a good self-image, nurtured by a loving family, and I felt confident that I could probably handle whatever lay ahead.

With regard to self-image, the way I saw my priestly persona was at once central to how I would undertake this new ministry and perhaps not so far from the perceptions many American priests of that time had of themselves. (This priestly self-image, I believe, is still very much with us.) As a fairly typical North American clergyman I saw myself as the "nice guy" who would influence people with an outgoing personality, together with genuine pastoral concern and attention. I would be the principal "cheerleader" for the new parish community, a propagandist for God and for the local church being established in the area assigned to us by the hierarchy of Lima. Later recollections by some of the original members of Most Holy Name verified the image I had of myself. They remembered the young American priest who showed up one day and began to make friends with everyone. The fact that I (sort of) played the guitar, they recalled, reinforced my image as a kind of clerical "Joe Cool" in the eyes of those early parishioners. (I relate this matter of self-image with some embarrassment, because in retrospect the "nice guy" approach to the pastoral situation I was thrown into had severe drawbacks, as will become abundantly clear as the story of Most Holy Name Parish unfolds.)

Everything in my background, especially my formation in religious life and priesthood, had pointed me in this pastoral direction. The best of pre-Vatican II seminary training, especially in the United States, emphasized the personal touch in its clergy and our approach to ministry. Not incidentally, we were told that this emphasis was the way to avoid the deadening anti-clericalism which gripped other countries of the world. ("There has to be clericalism before there is anti-clericalism" was the way they put it.) In our Franciscan training we heard over and over that kindliness had to be one of the highest priorities for a priest: "Treat people as you would want your mother treated." We had a very good model for ministry, but it was so incomplete. It was totally on the level of care for each individual, lacking in any social analysis or the challenges of the church's social teaching. It would be only very slowly that these broader ideas and prophetic ways of ministering would change and expand me and many others of our generation—but change and expand us they would.

I don't remember feeling any serious misgivings as those very early weeks and months of Most Holy Name Parish unfolded, except a sense that there would probably be too few hours in each day to accomplish everything that had to be done. In this and in many other ways I was typical of most missionaries coming from the United States to Latin America during that period.

A Significant Moment in History

As the parish got underway early in 1964 the church in Peru was functioning as it had for centuries. It was Eurocentric, still very much in the mold of the Spanish culture, in particular, and of theological approaches which the colonizers had brought in the fifteenth and sixteenth centuries. Soon after the Second Vatican Council ended, for example, the cardinal of Lima invited dozens of Spanish priests to conduct a city-wide mission. One of them told me that as they took off from the airport in Madrid these modern "conquistadors" sang in unison a traditional hymn to Mary. They were going to bring the Cross to "New Spain," as their forebears had done ever since the time of Columbus. Not surprisingly, as it turned out, that mission pretty much failed. An era was fast coming to an end.

During this time the Peruvian church was increasingly influenced for better or worse by the growing influx of religious and clergy from the United States and Canada. At a meeting on the campus of Notre Dame University in 1962, a representative from the Vatican called on North American religious congregations to send ten percent of their personnel to Latin America. The Holy See, it was said, was worried about the scarcity of native-born religious and priests in Central and South America and thought they saw a solution in the overflow of religious and priestly vocations then at their peak in North America. One U.S. prelate put the problem and the solution in terms of specific—and outlandish—numbers. 70,000 clergy and religious would be needed to "save" Latin America, he said. (What we were "saving" it from was not all that clear. However, communism certainly had to have been very much in his mind.)

Beginning in the early 60s, then, sisters, brothers and priests from the United States and Canada poured into the countries to the south, bringing with us many of the good aspects of our home churches and much that was less favorable. We arrived in Latin America with great enthusiasm and genuine concern for the people we had come to serve, qualities which made us welcome as we took up ministries all across the continent. However, most of us North Americans tended to judge success in quantitative terms—buildings constructed, numbers of people attending Mass and receiving the sacraments, the multiplication of catechetical programs. But many of us had little or no preparation for the culture of Latin America, and it was not uncommon to see good-willed sisters, priests and brothers from the north attempting to replicate the United States church in the new environment.

An exaggerated example of this religious imposition came to my attention while still in Bolivia. An Irish-born priest from a diocese in the U.S. told a group of us that he really didn't need to learn Spanish. "I thunder out the Ten Commandments in English," he said, fully expecting, it seemed, that the decibel level of his preaching would offset any language barrier. The same man spoke of sitting on a white horse at the head of annual St. Patrick's Day parades around his rural village. As noted, his case was an exaggeration, but one which points up the problems connected with throwing numbers of foreigners at complicated cultural situations.

The futility of this numbers solution to Latin American problems did not escape observation. Efforts were made, principally by the legendary Monsignor Ivan Illich at an orientation center in Ponce, Puerto Rico, later moved to Cuernavaca, Mexico, to prepare the growing numbers of missioners from the North with language skills and cultural sensitivities. A lesser-known center began in Brazil under the guidance of a veteran Franciscan missioner from the U.S., John Baptist Vogel. These initiatives met with modest success in sensitizing some of the large numbers of North American church people heading south into entirely different social and ecclesial realities.

Illich's approach was born of his own multicultural background and a natural sense of respect for culture, together with a horror at what he saw as yet another imposition of foreign religiosity on people who were already oppressed. His in-your-face courses on topics like "Cultural Imperialism" in Ponce and Cuernavaca shook to their roots many of the fairly naïve North Americans who had volunteered to "save" Latin America. The Monsignor also alienated U.S. and Canadian religious leaders in particular through a scathing article published in the Jesuit weekly *America* magazine, entitled "The Seamy Side of Charity." In it he seriously questioned the attempt to populate the church in Latin America with foreign personnel. There is a famous picture of Cardinal Richard Cushing of Boston waving a rolled up a copy of *America* as he railed against Illich's criticism. The Monsignor did not remain long in the hierarchy's good graces and eventually left the priesthood to engage in other pursuits.

A more creative response to the arrival of the North Americans came from the South, where some of the more insightful Latin American religious decided to welcome the "gringos" and convert us from unreflective proponents of a North American style church and society to critical social analysts, fully in touch with both Latin American realities and with the enormous influence of the United States on those realities. It was said that in answer to Illich's concern about the North American religious avalanche falling on the church in the south, the "Latinos" told him: "Let them come and we'll convert them and send them back to change North America." For many of us, their strategy worked very well.

Due to a lack of preparation and the unrealistic goals set for them, a large number of the religious and priests who had been inspired by the Vatican's call to service in Latin America returned to the U.S. after a few years, disillusioned with the frustrations of living and working in an unfamiliar and, to their minds, hostile environment. Still, despite their shortcomings, many of the North American religious who went to Latin America got high marks for pastoral and educational initiatives that were proving popular there. The parish schools headed by North American religious women became wildly popular with the local people, as did the range of spiritual and social activities which the U.S.-type parish provided for every age group in the community. In many places, the people thought of a parish as successful or not according to how it compared with those run by the North Americans.

Another factor which favored the numerous American missioners arriving in Latin America during those years of the early 60s was the "Kennedy phenomenon." The young Catholic president was greatly loved by the Latinos, who thought of him as their friend as well as a fellow church-member. Kennedy's assassination in November 1963 intensified for a time feelings of good will toward this country and the religious from here who were moving into Latin America.

A strange little meeting I had with an influential Spanish-born priest of the Lima Archdiocese within days after my arrival in Peru underscored for me this attraction of our North American way of parish life. Without much of an introduction, he gave me what amounted to a command that I immediately begin a parish school at Most Holy Name. He knew that the style of parish I had come to start would have its parochial school, conducted by U.S. sisters, and he had taken the liberty to promise some of his wealthy friends several coveted placements for their children in its first classrooms. The priest went so far as to hand me a list of their names.

I objected, telling him that starting the parish community was my first order of business and that the school would come only later. Incredibly, the Spaniard took the matter all the way to the cardinal and when the cardinal questioned me about it, I repeated my order of priorities and that any move toward a parochial school would follow as part of the overall parish plan. The prelate agreed and I heard no more from the Spanish priest or his friends. However, the experience highlights the popularity of our pastoral approaches, as well as the expectations placed on arriving U.S. religious and clergy.

It was into this historic reality that I stepped during that Peruvian summer of 1964. Indeed, I was part of it.

First Steps: Construction

The inaugural Mass described above was a direct result of consultations I had with several veteran Maryknoll missioners upon my arrival in Lima. It seemed a most natural thing that I should check with that group's sisters, priests and brothers before beginning the work at Most Holy Name. The Maryknollers already had years of experience in Latin America after their dismissal from Japanese-occupied China in the 1940s, and later from China under the communists. They established missions—U.S.-style for sure—in many rural areas of Latin America and in cities like Lima. For this young Franciscan, a visit to Maryknoll pastors in the three parishes they conducted in Lima was a must—and I was not disappointed. One of them took me on a kind of reconnaissance trip around the extensive area of my new parish, pointing out places where I might eventually build satellite chapels. When I asked a second Maryknoller what was the first thing I should do as the founding pastor of a parish, he advised me to build a makeshift altar where the parish center would later stand and begin celebrating the Eucharist for the parishioners. I followed this advice to the letter.

Guided by the advice and example of these long-time missioners, I sketched out in my mind the construction timetable I would follow. First of all, there was a mandate from my superiors in New York to build a combination parish house and rest-and-recreation facility for our Bolivian missioners. Next I would begin the construction of the parish school, adding classrooms as needed. This undertaking would be followed immediately by a parish center for the celebration of Sunday Mass as well as for the various parish gatherings which would follow. I was confident that this building program would serve as the basic infrastructure for the first years of Most Holy Name. These various construction projects, undertaken in the first year, would also indicate clearly, I felt, that these Franciscans from the United States were serious about our new parish venture.

The North American religious who went to Central and South America during those years arrived with significant economic backing from their dioceses and congregations back home, enough money to support all their pastoral initiatives—many of which were not needed. Someone said years later that the Latin American landscape was dotted with buildings erected by these North American missioners, representing resources which might better have gone to more pressing human needs.

While understandable in light of enormous enthusiasm and support in the U.S. for the hundreds of clergy and religious answering the Vatican's call to "save" Latin America, the injection of large sums of money into the church there on the part of the foreigners was questionable on at least two counts. First, it made us look to the local people very much like our U.S. counterparts in the business and political world—sort of ecclesiastical high-rollers with deep pockets. Far from behaving as servant-missioners who had come to do what might be asked of us by the local church, most of us arrived on the scene like religious entrepreneurs, constructing and presiding over impressive physical plants. Second, the resources available to the U.S. missioners tended to diminish the poorer and materially limited Latin American religious and clergy in the eyes of the people. This had repercussions on many levels: it led to something of a fascination with the "big spenders" from the North and perhaps to some lessening of respect for the national church people; it risked making the "North American" (read upwardly mobile) form of priesthood and religious life very attractive to young Latinos who might be considering such a vocation; and finally, it tended to engender in us missioners a sense of accomplishment based more on "brick and mortar" than on pastoral considerations.

In the matter of full economic support from the U.S., Holy Name Parish was no exception. Even before the first parish Mass, I had already commissioned a noted Peruvian architect to draw plans for a parish house, to be followed by outlines of the first classrooms for the parochial school and a large all-purpose auditorium. These were my initiatives. Neither the fifty or so families who made up the new parish, nor even the church hierarchy had any say in these undertakings. The money came from my Franciscan sponsors in New York and I felt free to dispense it as I saw fit. No one challenged the arrangement.

I think back on this system of absolute autonomy and I cringe. What a violation of local sensitivities and of the local church! Where did I, where did any of us North Americans, get the right to roll into the Latin American church scene and implement our ideas and plans regarding the religious expressions of those unique faith communities? Yet I do not remember any discussions among us of the anomaly we represented. Nor did any challenge come from church officials where I was. They seemed to accept my high-handed way of proceeding as a price to be paid for the "benefit" of having our community serve there. And besides, what I was doing at Most Holy Name in forging ahead on my own with construction projects, my fellow American missioners were doing all around me.

First Steps: Pastoral

In addition to the building program, I had the goal—really much more important to me—of getting acquainted with every household in the parish. My daily routine during those first weeks and months always included time to drop in on the families living within the geographical limits of Most Holy Name, with special attention to new arrivals. At first these informal and spontaneous visits seemed to come as a surprise, even as an intrusion, for the more sophisticated social sector of the parish population, who, as we shall see, made up a significant portion of the parishioners. The middle and upper middle class of Peru operated with considerable formality in its business and social dealings. One usually phoned, wrote a note or sent a *tarjeta* (business card) to inquire about the feasibility and convenience of a visit on a certain day and hour. On many occasions during those ground-breaking months in Most Holy Name I would be greeted at the door or on the intercom of a parishioner's home with: "What is it that you want?" or even more pointedly the maid would inform me that "the Señora says she is not at home." Gradually, however, the impromptu visits of the new North American pastor became an acceptable, even sought-after, part of parish life. More important, I succeeded in getting to know virtually every person in Most Holy Name Parish by name. My "nice guy" reputation began to soar.

At that point in my personal history, and indeed in that of most American religious and clergy in Latin America, any prophetic or conflictive role—one which might challenge lifestyles or social structures—remained entirely outside of my field of vision. The occasional exception to this unquestioning and increasingly popular expression of ministry would show itself when the need arose to deal with the occasional "stray sheep" who needed a little push toward Mass attendance or reception of the sacraments. However, my overriding pastoral concern remained on the level of personal morality, each one's relationship with God through the church.

In the light of the subsequent historic events which would overtake the Peruvian church and Most Holy Name during the next eleven years, my memories of this traditional and intensely personalistic be-

ginning seem remote, strange, even somewhat incredible. Still, seeds
were sown at the beginning which would later bear fruit in ways no
one could have imagined in those first weeks and months. The new
parish had no entrenched traditions or customs to change or overcome—it was all new, everything was a fresh start. One significant
segment of the parishioners, including the pastor, was made up of
young middle-class folks, open to new ways of experiencing church.
The reduced numbers of parishioners at the start gave the parish a
wonderful sense of community, where everyone knew each other's
name. And the hierarchy of the church in Lima, out of conviction or
necessity, maintained a "hands-off" policy and an attitude which, for
all the abdication of responsibility it represented, allowed for a climate of freedom as Most Holy Name Parish began to take shape.

CHAPTER 2

Social Analysis

My very first visit to a home in the new parish brought me into contact with one of the three distinct social sectors that made up Most Holy Name. The door was opened by a young woman, dressed in a smock, who identified herself as a maid in the household. She seemed quite at ease as she answered my questions about her employers and their children. We chatted in the doorway for some time (the owners were not home at the moment and an employee would have no authority to admit anyone into the house) and I found that the young woman, whose name was Cristina, had come from the Andean highlands of Peru to the capital in search of a better life. Despite an obvious native intelligence, her lack of education and—more important—her inferior social standing as a *serrana* (an Indian woman from the high country) meant that the best she could aspire to was employment as a live-in domestic servant. It turned out that Cristina was representative of hundreds like her, with similar backgrounds and history, who found themselves working for middle- and upper-middle-class families in Lima and the other cities of Peru. One demographer estimated that four or five domestics worked in each household. What was unique about Cristina was her ease in conversing with me. I soon found that the majority of her fellow domestic workers had extremely inferior self-images.

A second social level in the parish was that represented by Cristina's employers, the masters and mistresses of the homes where she and the other domestics worked and lived. In the Lima area at that time these middle- and upper-middle-class families were moving in large numbers from the older, somewhat declining center city to American-type suburbs. They were usually young well-educated professionals who through family connections and personal industriousness had already achieved a measure of security and comfort and they considered themselves entitled to continue this upwardly mobile trajectory in their own lives and those of their children. The move to new subdivisions like the one which would be served by Most Holy Name was a significant measure of their growing success.

A third segment of the parish began to enter my field of vision as I started making my daily rounds. These were the often overlooked or ignored caretakers of the large number of homes being constructed all across the area of the parish. Called *guardianes*, or caretakers, they usually lived with their families, at the pleasure of the building contractor, in squalid shacks located on each new housing lot. In addition to the menial construction work they did by day, the caretakers were charged with warding off thefts of building materials during the off hours. When a house was completed and the middle-class owners moved in, the caretaker and his family got assigned—if they were so fortunate—to a new construction site and the cycle would begin all over again. Otherwise they joined the thousands of unemployed and underemployed who thronged the streets of Lima begging passersby or shop owners to give them some little task for which they hoped to receive payment enough to survive yet another day.

A year or so after the inauguration of Most Holy Name I commissioned a team from the local Catholic university to do a sociological study of the parish. The results confirmed my initial perception of the tri-level social makeup of the parish.

I believe that consideration of these three sociological sectors is in order now even though these details and nuances only gradually penetrated my consciousness and that of the other U.S. Franciscans who began to join me. For during the first many months we felt our first obligation to be that of providing an infrastructure for parish life, and at the same time developing—principally among the middle and upper middle class, it must be admitted—enthusiasm for their new parish community. Little else occupied us during those early and obviously busy times. Nevertheless, a slightly more detailed analysis of the complex social makeup of Most Holy Name Parish will be useful in understanding the dramatic story of the parish as it unfolded.

Domestic Servants

The domestic servants lived lives of complete, almost slave-like dependence on their employers. Like young Cristina, my first contact among them, they had little or no education. The great majority were Indian women and men who had left their homes in the rural areas of Peru to seek a way out of the continuous cycle of poverty into which they had been born, only to encounter an even more grinding urban impoverishment in the capital city of Lima and other urban centers of Peru. Still, they continued to migrate toward the cities, hoping against hope that somehow they might find a way to break out of their economic enslavement, particularly through education.

Without the skills necessary for productive work in the modern urban centers to which they migrated, they wound up eking out an existence in the homes of the privileged classes, often sleeping on a folding cot in the kitchen or, at best, in substandard quarters behind the house, eating the leftovers from the family's table. They worked long hours every day, beginning with the preparation of the family's breakfast early in the morning and often ending only when they opened the garage doors for the homeowners arriving from some social gathering late at night. The domestic workers received meager salaries, since the homeowners felt that they were doing them a great favor simply by offering them "room and board." The servants knew, and were constantly reminded, that they remained in the household particularly at the pleasure of the lady of the house. Any complaints about working conditions, displays of fatigue or requests for days off, vacations or schooling were met with stern warnings and sometimes outright dismissal. They all knew that there were far more workers seeking jobs than positions to fill.

The situation of the domestic workers underscored the rigid social castes of Peruvian society. It was not only the lack of education which bound these young women and men to their menial, denigrating work situations. They were shackled also by what one Peruvian observer described as the "backdrop of racism" behind the country's social stratification. In the first years of Most Holy Name I attended the wife and mother of a middle-class family during the last months of a fatal illness. Knowing she would not survive to bring up her several young children, the woman with exceptional foresight prepared one of her domestics to take over the household. She chose well, for the girl showed great talent for managing the home, and the children already had respect and love for their "second mother." She was also quite beautiful and, thanks to training on the part of her sick and dying employer, refined and well-spoken. However, after the woman passed away and her widower began to seek a spouse and stepmother for his children, no consideration whatsoever was given to this employee: she was still a *serrana*, still an Indian. There was simply no way the widower could possibly marry so far below his station. In fact, the young woman finally had to seek employment elsewhere because with her proven skills and closeness to the children, she represented a rival and a threat to the new, socially acceptable lady of the house.

Middle and Upper-Middle Class

For their part the middle- and upper-middle-class homeowners populating the new parish lived lives of privilege in every sense of the word. Through a unique network of family and "old boy" school connections to many others of their influential class, the men held well-paid positions in the professions, the business world, in politics or the military, complete with such perks as access to exclusive clubs, in some cases chauffeured cars, and the ever-present *bara* (political, economic or social influence and "pull" within their peer group). While not part of Peru's landed aristocracy (more on that class later), the comfortable privileged middle class imitated the lives of the super-wealthy. Most of them traveled abroad with some frequency; they conversed easily on a variety of national and international subjects, ate at exclusive restaurants and enjoyed posh beach clubs. They increasingly learned to speak English and generally exhibited a cosmopolitan, worldly attitude toward life.

A vivid, though quite negative, example of this lifestyle occurred on one occasion around an attempt by a middle-class man and woman, one of whom had been married previously, to get me to celebrate their second marriage—something the Catholic Church would not permit. When I discovered the couple's deceit in swearing to their status as single people and halted the process, the would-be bride's father asked to speak with me. He began in English, an obvious ploy to ingratiate himself with the gringo pastor. After I insisted on carrying on our conversation in Spanish, he proceeded to ask blatantly: "Between two men of the world, how much would I need to give you to celebrate the marriage?" I ended the conversation right there. Next day the local newspapers carried a small notice that such and such a wedding had to be postponed due to the bride's "indisposition." That sad little story underscored for me some of the negative aspects of this tight middle-class society in Lima.

The homes of this rising class, especially those being built in areas such as Most Holy Name Parish, reflected their affluence and a typically Latin American emphasis on living life principally within one's family and tight social circle. All their houses had exterior walls with formidable gates and impressive, if often crude, systems of security—glass shards imbedded in the tops of the walls or attack dogs stationed—of all places—on the rooftops. The clear message was that outsiders were unwelcome. Inside the homes, spacious and well-appointed rooms on the first floor led to interior patios, which often featured small swimming pools. Upstairs, each member of the family had his or her own room with adjacent bathroom. Since the temperate climate of Lima eliminated the necessity for central heating and air conditioning, the family could spend money on marble or parquet floors, expensive wall hangings and vases. The furniture, frequently custom-made, served to highlight and complement the aura of wealth and privilege.

Certain formalities, some exaggerated and some quite congenial, regulated the lives of the Peruvian middle class and added to their sense of status and superiority over the "lower class" folks. The *tarjeta* held much importance both for the donor and the recipient, as it signaled the bearer's membership in the old boy network, thereby promising access to the *bara* mentioned above. Dropping in unannounced at a person's home was not considered good form (though, as mentioned, from the beginning, I tended to apply a dose of North American brashness and ignore the required appointment, deciding that there simply was not enough time to be bothered with such niceties in my daily unstructured rounds). If such a visit did happen to take place, the householders attended graciously to the guest, even to the point of foregoing previously scheduled engagements. One cultural amenity I quickly learned was to determine if the family did indeed have plans pending, in which case I would cut the visit short. Otherwise, Peruvian protocol would insist that the family entertain me for as long as I "graced" their home. There was an almost excessive concern for personal hygiene with these upper-middle-class folks, and table manners held a high place in their eyes. Such graceful gestures as waiting until everyone had been served at table before beginning one's meal were a must.

For the women of the upper-middle class, marriage was crucial. Girls were educated from their earliest years for the comfortable status which a well-connected marriage would afford them. Once married, these pampered women spent their days "managing" the household by overseeing the work of their three, four or five domestic servants. They drove in their recent-model cars to a constant round of fiestas, teas and lunches during the day, careful always to arrive home before their husbands so as to present themselves as the attractive spouse, lady of the house, mother of his children when he came in after work or after his own social rounds. In a moment of unusual candor, one of these women told me that she was trapped in a gilded cage.

The wives' attitude toward their husbands was coquettish and subservient, sometimes to the point of humiliation, since they lived in fear of the double standard of morality within their class—strict fidelity to husband and family on the part of the women; license for the men to stray from their marriage vows. A measure of this uneven and unjust morality would arise on the rare occasion when a woman might violate her marriage commitment. She would live thereafter with a soiled reputation. Her husband, in contrast, was granted great latitude in his extra-marital escapades. I always felt these upper-middle-class wives were women of considerable charm and beauty, but with a few notable exceptions they lived lives of crushing boredom or, at best, comfortable uselessness.

The children of these households received their education in the context and in function of this social reality. All went to private, mostly

Catholic, schools, directed by Peruvian or European priests and nuns, where the students established the connections within their class which would be to their advantage for the rest of their lives. A few American congregations engaged in this ministry of private education, subscribing to the theory that the conversion of Latin America could come through proper training of the privileged classes. However, these were the exception among the U.S. missioners who flocked to Central and South America in those years. (More about this when I describe the dilemma in which we found ourselves with regard to the parish school at Most Holy Name.)

The upper-middle-class boys were not expected to hold jobs outside of school or even do chores around the house; they had all of their needs taken care of by the domestic workers or their mothers and sisters, a situation which would continue when they established their own homes. The girls lived similarly privileged lives, except for the fact that they always took second place after their brothers and later after their husbands. The young people of the family took the inferior status of the domestic workers in the household for granted and treated them with tolerance, even disdain, from their earliest years.

On a visit to the United States during these years I had the occasion to eat lunch at a restaurant with a family from the parish who were visiting the U.S. I pointed out to their teenage daughter that our waiter was a student at a local prestigious university. Her reaction was total incomprehension: "What is he doing that for?"

As the product of a different, more democratic, American middle class, I found myself put off by these family systems on my visits to their mini-mansions. I realized that they represented a culture which did not easily lend itself to communal values like neighborhood or parish identity. Everything about them pointed to a family and social life lived within the walls, exclusionary even of their next-door neighbors. Early conversations with parishioners touched on the reality of their middle-class exclusivity and I often sensed that they believed my efforts at building community would not work. However, I also knew that these young middle-class men and women were open to new ideas, and I resolved to make the parish a place where they and their families would feel welcome and part of a larger whole. I felt this was part of the mission entrusted to us.

Caretakers

The families on the lowest rung of this social ladder, the caretakers at the building sites that dotted the parish area, presented a reality dramatically opposite from that of the people whose homes they were protecting during the period of construction. These were the poorest of the poor. Their menfolk—numerous, unskilled and uneducated laborers—vied for the scarce, entry-level jobs available in this growing subdivision. Like the domestic servants, the caretakers knew very well that they could lose their jobs at a moment's notice. Thus, there was to be no complaining about their harsh working and living conditions, no appeal to the relatively progressive Peruvian labor laws in case of injury or suspension of work, and above all no trespassing or lost materials on the construction site.

For the most part these men accepted their inferior situation unquestioningly. I came to know one of the caretakers fairly well during my daily round of parish visits. The man lived alone on the site of what was shaping up to be an unusually large and elaborate home even for that area. One day I asked him about his own home and learned that the man's family lived quite a distance away, in extremely poor circumstances. Did he, I asked, see any discrepancy between his family's living situation and the exclusive home which was under construction before his eyes. "No, that's just the way it is," he answered, "these are the big people."

The wives of the caretakers did their best to ease their husbands' burden by seeking work of their own—the occasional opportunity to wash clothes for a wealthy family or sell cigarettes and newspapers to commuters at bus stops early in the morning. These understanding and long-suffering women also put up with the frequent despair-induced alcoholic excesses of their husbands. They knew that life and society had dealt their men a dreadful hand and they felt that the safety valve of a husband's weekly drunk was not the end of the world for them or the family. Unfortunately, however, in addition to depleting a family's meager income, this masculine despair would often take the form of physical abuse toward the wives and children. Not infrequently, desperation drove the menfolk to simply walk out on their families, leaving the women and children in even more desperate straits.

Long before I heard the term "the feminization of poverty," I knew what it looked like. The poorest women of Peru carried their impoverished class on their backs. An example helps underscore this observation and something of the responsibility which the menfolk among the wretchedly poor carried for these conditions.

Late one night I took a sick child and her mother to a local hospital for emergency treatment. (These trips became more and more common as the parish developed and the very poor came to know us Franciscans.) In the waiting area sat another extremely poor woman with a sick baby in her arms, accompanied by a nine-year-old daughter. After the usual lengthy wait both infants finally received attention and were ready to be discharged about the same time. I asked the second woman how far away she lived and learned that it was some six or seven miles to her home. At that late hour the buses had stopped running and I knew she would have to walk, so I identified myself as a priest and offered to drive her and the children home. She was only too happy to accept.

On the way I asked where the woman's husband was and she told me he was home in bed. My next question was a logical one: "Is his work so physically demanding that he needs all the rest he can get?" The woman answered that her husband had lost his job and was out of work. "Who supports your family, then?" I asked. " I do," came the reply, "by selling cigarettes, gum and newspapers at the train stop early each morning." The woman saw absolutely no contradiction in this situation, herself shouldering all of the family's burdens while her husband did nothing, not even accompanying her on a late night visit to the hospital. Hers was a similar reaction to that of the watchman who said: "That's just the way it is."

The children of these oppressed and marginalized families reared themselves as best they could. Parental affection and oversight were at a minimum due to the parents' grinding impoverishment and total absence of leisure. A deficient, erratic public school system was all that was available for their educational needs, and the children themselves had to make their contribution to the struggle for survival which confronted their families every day.

One of my most unforgettable experiences was the one I described in the introduction of this book. I accompanied the Valencia family during the days following the death of nine-year-old José, who was struck down by a hit-and-run driver as he walked home with a cooking pot full of food begged from the middle-class families in the parish. Despite being a pupil in our parochial school, José was not a good student. For one thing, he was chronically hungry; he could count on little or no supervision from his illiterate and overburdened parents; and even his physical surroundings—the shack that was his home, with no electricity and close living quarters—all combined to hold this unfortunate lad back in the one area which might have given him and his family a way out of their poverty—education. One night, about eleven o'clock, I saw one of our poor little boys sitting on the curb outside of the crowded hovel which substituted for a house, studying by the only light available: a street lamp.

Oligarchy

There was another social class in Peru, one which had little effect on Most Holy Name Parish except in the very beginning and on a few occasions thereafter, consisting of the landed aristocracy, the fabulously rich owners of immense productive tracts of land (*haciendas*) all over Peru. I mention them to fill out the picture of the Peruvian social strata and to illustrate the sort of lifestyle which many middle- and upper-middle-class Peruvians imitated. These were the Rockefellers or Carnegies of that country.

One of these families, the Castañedas, actually owned the huge area where the new parish would be established and were carving it into lots at enormous profit. Appreciating the advertising benefit the North American priests and, later, the teaching sisters represented, they offered the archdiocese a full city block of land on which to situate the parish buildings. For the family the donation was a wise business deal, because a flourishing parish would stimulate sales of the house lots in the large subdivision they owned, a fact which I somewhat cynically pointed out to my New York superiors when they waxed eloquent over the "generosity" of this "very Catholic" family.

Within a week of my arrival in Lima I was knocking at the door of the Castañeda mansion in an older section of the city—having first made an appointment—in order to talk about the transfer of their land donation to the parish. A male servant, complete with white coat, black trousers and highly polished shoes, ushered me into a drawing room to await the master of the house, Don Armando. After some pleasantries between the old man and me, we adjourned to a formal dining room for tea, served by similarly clothed house-boys sporting immaculate white gloves. At the table Mr. Castañeda signed over something in the vicinity of $200,000 worth of land with a flourish of his gold pen. For this son of Irish immigrants, it was a world I had only read about. Yet I cannot say that I was intimidated or overwhelmed by it all. I'm sure my American democratic convictions kicked in at that point. Nevertheless, it was an oligarchy with its extreme wealth on display.

Seated at the table that afternoon were two other priests, older men, whose purpose in asking for an "audience" with Don Armando struck me as bordering on the bizarre. After he and I had finished our land deal, these clerical gentlemen began to push the old hacienda owner for dates when work would be suspended on the plantation and they could "evangelize," that is, baptize, marry and give First Communion to the workers and their families. After this brief sacramental vacation, of course, the workers would return to the near-slavelike lives they normally lived. The priests reminded Mr. Castañeda that he had set aside time for this spiritual work on many occasions in the past and it was time to do so again. I couldn't believe what I was hearing and at a lull in the conversation brashly interjected that I thought we were living in the twentieth century but from what I was hearing it felt more like the sixteenth.

Not long after the parish was founded, an elderly Spanish Franciscan showed up at Most Holy Name in the Castañeda's chauffeured Mercedes-Benz automobile. The friar introduced himself as the family's chaplain and explained that he would soon have to relinquish this ministry due to advancing age. He went on to say that the family had taken notice of me during the negotiations around the transfer of their land donation to Most Holy Name and wished to invite me to serve as the new chaplain. Evidently I had made some-

thing of a favorable impression, despite my views on religious observances at the hacienda. According to this friar, the duties would con-
sist of an occasional Mass in the private chapel of the Castañeda home,
celebration on request of other sacraments and generally serving as
spiritual guide for what the older Franciscan called this "very Catholic family." In return, I would have use of the Mercedes (when the
family did not need it), and support for all of my "charities"—a eu-
phemism for any poor people I might run across in the course of my
ministry.

I reacted with genuine astonishment that the old system of religious catering in this way to the extremely wealthy still continued. I
politely but very firmly refused to consider the offer. My task in Lima,
I told him, was to launch a parish, not serve one rich family. The
older priest shook his head, unable to comprehend what he considered an incredible missed opportunity on the part of this young American pastor. These were my first encounters with what I considered
deadening pastoral situations in which church people placed themselves in a position of courtiers to the wealthy and powerful, while
snatching at the few crumbs the rich might throw them from their
opulent tables. The picture struck me as dated, ugly and harmful to
the church's mission.

Unfortunately, the phenomenon of gospel ministers at the service
of the status quo in Latin America was not limited to the occasional
chaplain to an aristocratic family. At that time, the entire Latin American institutional church, especially its hierarchical dimensions, projected this bias in favor of the entrenched upper classes. In fact, for
centuries the church served as the legitimizing, even spiritualizing,
force in a triumvirate which included the church, the oligarchy and
the near-absolute political/military power which kept the whole unjust system in place, to the extreme detriment of millions living subhuman lives. Fortunately, the Latin American church was to call itself to a new moment and a new reality within a very short time.

The sociological study mentioned above and the insights it provided into the different classes of people residing in Most Holy Name
reinforced my initial instinct that continued reflection on the social
realities of the parish, and of the city and country as well, would be
essential to my pastoral role and responsibilities. As time went on,

this social analysis became a daily part of life in the parish, the principal tool which set the course for what Most Holy Name would become. In fact, the conviction grew within all of us who engaged in the life of the new parish that without ongoing reflection on the socioeconomic dimensions of any such ecclesial entity, truly effective pastoral work would be impossible.

CHAPTER 3

The Early Years

Building the Infrastructure

A mandate I received on being sent to begin the new parish followed directly from one of the reasons my Franciscan province in New York had for taking a parish in Lima. They wanted a rest and recreation center for our men working in the taxing climate and environs of our Bolivian mission. Many of the young American friars who had gone to Bolivia were forced to return home due to a range of physical, emotional and mental problems directly attributable to the harshness of life in that country. (Before my time in Bolivia every one of my brother Franciscans had suffered bouts of hepatitis, many others got malaria and at least two left the country after severe mental breakdowns.)

On arriving in Peru, therefore, I knew that my first task was to build a combination parish and vacation house as soon as possible for us friars who would be assigned to the parish and for the Bolivian missioners to stay at during what was called their "altitude leave." So a few days after flying into Lima I met with a group of American sisters who were building a large educational complex outside the city and then I contacted their architect to ask him to draw up plans for the new friary.

As noted, it was assumed by all—New York Franciscans, Lima's Archbishop and of course the parishioners—that, as a parish in the American model, Most Holy Name would have a parochial school. I instructed the architect, in addition to the plans for the parish and recreation houses, that he begin general sketches for the first of the school's classrooms.

It was clear from the housing starts in the area that before long the numbers of parishioners moving into the new subdivision that was Most Holy Name Parish would require a large gathering place for Sunday Eucharist and their other spiritual, educational and social functions. So a third task was assigned to the architect—to plan an auditorium which could be used for these several purposes.

(I explicitly ruled out any consideration of a church building at this early stage. That felt to me like a luxury at the moment and something we could deal with as time went on. The issue of the church would become something of a difficulty between the cardinal and me later on.)

Monies for the friary would come from the Franciscan province in New York, since the building was designed for our men. Loans from the province would finance the other buildings, although the terms of amortization remained vague, perhaps because of the enthusiasm for the new venture among the Franciscans in New York. The entire financial arrangement for the new parish at this point copied exactly what so many American missioners to South and Central America were enjoying—a kind of carte blanche for our building decisions without much oversight on the part of the home office or requirement of accountability from me.

It was a loose system, but I gave myself high marks in one area, at least. As monies from New York began to arrive, I learned that Peru had a surcharge of 10% on every check in dollars cashed in the country. There was logic to this tax. If foreign private enterprise was investing and making huge profits in Peru, the country had a right to some of that initial investment. However, I felt that we Franciscans were bringing in money without any profit motive. It was capital that would remain in the country long after we had left. I felt justified in finding a legal means to circumvent the surcharge by cashing our checks through a multinational corporation which was for some reason legally exempt from the tax, thus saving us thousands of dollars.

My philosophy and mode of operating with regard to this initial quite ambitious building program was what would be described as "laid back." I felt I had consulted the right people—in this case, a successful group of American missionary sisters with experience in the country—and had chosen a competent professional to plan these buildings. Except for an occasional check on the architect's progress, I stayed away from any micro-management of his work. In this case, however, I eventually had to second-guess myself. Within eight or nine months of initiating the planning stage of this building program, I felt obliged to take the unfinished projects out of the hands of the original architect. The man had proven competence in his field but turned out to be most unreliable in actually producing the finished plans needed to begin construction. This major decision to switch architects proved correct, as it speeded up progress on all of the planned buildings.

Just over a year after the inaugural Mass the first classrooms of the parish school were completed. A month later the parish and vacation houses opened and the all-purpose auditorium was blessed two years after that. In all of this, I gave minimum attention to the day-to-day construction. I felt confident in my judgment about those contracted to do the work and I tended to let them get on with it. In this the new architect and the builders did not disappoint. My hands-off attitude served as an indicator of my true interest—the pastoral, spiritual side of the new parish community. My priority in this regard was not the result of any special virtue of mine, except, perhaps, for an instinctive rejection of the building mentality I had seen in pastors during my growing up years in the United States. Aside from that, I felt that while I was a fair judge of the people I contracted to construct the buildings, I was almost completely ignorant of how buildings are put up. Playing the interfering boss was simply not my style. I was much more concerned about what I saw as the real task of a parish—personal contacts and the religious dimension of life. The arrangement worked well for all concerned—well-constructed buildings (in that earthquake-prone coastal area of Peru) and an immediate, sustained attention to the spiritual life of Most Holy Name on the part of its priest.

A Beginning Option

It was clear that the major pastoral thrust in the first years of Most Holy Name went in the direction of the middle- and upper-middle-class homeowners. Now I look back on this preference with some embarrassment, given the dire situations and pressing pastoral needs of the domestic servants and the caretakers in the parish. But at the time Most Holy Name got underway concentration on its middle-class members was perhaps an understandable, perhaps even an in-evitable choice for us. The privileged class in the parish was the most visible and influential, so we fell into that long-held conviction among Latin American church people that converting this class would even-tually mean the conversion of the whole society. (It didn't occur to me or, for that matter, to most of those engaged in church work there that this theory had held sway for centuries without any perceived movement toward social change.) More subjectively (selfishly?), for me and my brother American Franciscans who joined me, the middle-class folks were also the most congenial. Their wide experience, good manners and typical Latin graciousness described above were enor-mously attractive, so that it was natural for us foreign religious to gravitate personally, socially and, therefore, pastorally toward this class. On the other hand, the domestic servants and the caretakers exhib-ited more of a deferential, even subservient attitude, which in the beginning years of Most Holy Name was off-putting to us North Americans. It was much easier and inviting to hobnob with people who looked and acted like ourselves than to seek out the poorer folks.

The best example of the "good chemistry" which existed between the North American religious and the middle-class parishioners was my early and long-lasting friendship with one young professional and his family. When I came to know him, this man had already made a name for himself as a pioneer engineer of anti-seismic high-rise build-ings in that earthquake zone of Latin America. His expertise had developed through studies in Great Britain and the United States, something which made our friendship a natural, and one which grew and deepened as time went on. I enjoyed visiting his home, sharing the family's stereo system and well-stocked musical library, and above all conversing about national and international politics. As an avid student of the Second Vatican Council and later the implementation of Vatican II in the Latin American church, he became my chief ad-visor during the decade I served Most Holy Name Parish, helping me in a wide variety of ways to understand my role as a "Peruvian" pastor. Indeed, I later reflected that this Latin American professional was one of the best friends I have ever had.

Parish Work

With two brother Franciscans joining me, the first months and years of Most Holy Name saw an ever-expanding menu of spiritual services offered to the middle- and upper-middle-class parishioners. We celebrated Eucharist each morning in the large chapel of the newly built parish house and several Masses each Sunday in the all-purpose auditorium. We made sure that time for weddings and baptisms was readily available, often accommodating to the busy schedules of the middle-class parishioners. The constant round of house visits brought us into contact with elderly and sick parishioners to whom we subsequently brought the sacraments and other spiritual comforts. Hospital visits even to members of the parishioners' extended family became routine. A death in the family of a parish member automatically brought one of the Franciscans for the viewing and burial, as well as the celebration of a Mass of Resurrection on the eighth day after death, as was the Peruvian custom.

All of this pastoral outreach impressed and delighted the members of the new parish. During those early years the mother of a parishioner was diagnosed with terminal cancer. This lovely, pious woman lived in another parish and, as she became increasingly confined to her home, asked her family if a priest could be found to bring her daily Communion. The son and daughter-in-law who were members of Most Holy Name assured her with great pride that one of their priests would willingly perform this service—and so it was. Day after day for the several months of the woman's last illness I visited her with the Eucharist, and eventually assisted her and the family in her last hours and on through the funeral and burial. This pastoral outreach beyond the "boundaries" of Most Holy Name earned us, of course, the enormous gratitude and appreciation of the woman's entire family and they all joined Most Holy Name. For the Franciscans such ministerial attention was routine—we had been trained that way; among the people it was celebrated.

In addition to this full range of spiritual services and house visits, we participated in fiestas, birthday parties, wedding receptions, and the parish-sponsored social gatherings we began. The Franciscans became a familiar presence in virtually every social event celebrated by the growing number of families in the parish. Indeed it was not uncommon for us to join parishioners at dinners in local restaurants, quite a novelty as well as an honor for Peruvians at that time. When the parish grew to the point where getting to every social event became increasingly difficult due to the sheer numbers of parishioners, having one of the *padres* at one's home or out to dinner became something of a coup among this socially competitive class of people.

Within a few months of the first Sunday Eucharist, I began parish fiestas. These were all-expenses-paid (by the parish) dinner parties, often including live orchestras and dancing, open to all parishioners. My reasoning behind these popular events had much to do with the parishioners' tendency to live behind the walls of their comfortable homes, confining all social life to their own tight circles. I felt it was important to try to break open these little islands in order to foster a more communal spirit in Most Holy Name. Of course they became immensely popular and increasingly well-attended, until after a few years the parish grew to the point where the expense involved became unmanageable.

A small footnote to these parish-sponsored and other fiestas was my own participation. Along the way I had picked up rudimentary skills with the guitar, at least enough to accompany myself on a few songs (particularly in English). It became something of a highlight moment when this extroverted American priest would perform at the fiestas, especially in the eyes of teenagers in the parish who loved the guitar and American music.

Another non-spiritual but no less pastoral activity were the *paseos* (day trips) to the beach or other swimming areas which I took with a large number of children and young people during summer months. My own vitality at the time allowed me to serve as supervisor, lifeguard and referee in the water and beach games which these children and young adults played. Their parents, of course, found this sort of parish activity novel as well as incredibly attractive and welcome.

This style of parochial activities, with the clergy and later the sisters who came to run the parish school, engaged in all aspects of the community's life, proved innovative and immensely popular in the minds of the parishioners. In fact, it would be difficult to exaggerate the impact and the lasting importance which this entirely new approach to pastoral life and work had on Most Holy Name Parish. The Peruvian people, nearly all baptized Catholics, had generally experienced an older, more reserved, almost dour type of religious.

To be fair, the reduced number of local clergy and religious and their overwhelming work load (similar to what is happening today in the U.S. church) made it inevitable that our style of vigorous, all-out pastoral attention would not easily be replicated among them. I remember listening to one local priest as he described the grinding, seven-day weeks he put in as the only priest in a parish of 70,000 people. The poor man knew he was burned out. On one occasion he spent two weeks on vacation at our parish house, gradually recovering slightly from his mental and physical exhaustion. Upon leaving to take up his duties once again, he confided to me that in a day or two he would be right back into his usual weary, short-tempered ways with his people. Where could he ever find time or energy for a fiesta or a beach trip? It was precisely this scarcity of vocations and incredibly overworked ministers that had motivated the Vatican's historic call to America for help.

Similar situations in Peru and many other Latin American countries at that time meant that the priests generally could only be found behind the closed doors of the parish house or monastery, or on the run to ever-present emergency situations in the poor populations they served. They were therefore unfamiliar and somewhat forbidding figures, giving off an unspoken (or sometimes even spoken) attitude of aloofness and disinterest. In addition, the Peruvian clergy had to depend for much of their livelihood on stipends received for sacramental service. Their ministries, therefore, often seemed more like business transactions than pastoral opportunities. The personal and professional attitudes of such priests were most unpopular, especially with the young, up-and-coming middle class then emerging in Peru, though this was terribly unfair and there were some notable exceptions among the local clergy. We Americans, with our immense resources and opportunities for appropriate relaxation, including occasional vacations in the United States, looked very good by comparison.

The women religious in Peru, the *madrecitas* (little mothers), for the most part followed a similarly grim pattern. Theirs was a semicloistered life, working in large private schools or with needy elderly people or orphans, for which they received much gratitude but not much support from the populace. Like the priests, the local sisters lived lives that were almost entirely removed from what was regarded by the people as normalcy, expected to spend long hours in prayer and bound by vows and customs which confined them in every way. The occasional conversation between a lay Peruvian and these priests and sisters perforce centered on religious matters. It was as if the people believed that church persons could not address or understand anything but "spiritual" topics.

This description of the local priests and sisters in Peru at that time refers to a pre-Vatican II generation with all of the limitations which that era of church life placed on its vowed and clerical members. Very little consideration was given in those days to such human requirements as psychological health, the need for intimacy, or time for oneself. The thinking, particularly in Latin American religious circles, held that prayer and one's spiritual life should suffice for healthy and pastorally productive lives—a patently wrong understanding of basic human requirements.

Of course there were exceptions to these general observations regarding the lives and customs of local Peruvian priests and religious of that time. By the grace of God and sheer personal giftedness, some church people did seem to live happy and fulfilled lives. And as time went on and the effects of Second Vatican Council took hold, a renewed, progressive and dynamic generation of clergy and religious gradually took their place in the Peruvian church. More about them later. What is significant here is that when Most Holy Name Parish began, we Franciscans and later on the religious women who served there represented a breath of new life that was uncommon in Peru at that time and most attractive to the Peruvian people. We appeared to be everything that the majority of their own church people were not— young, friendly, free of a deadening "cloister mentality," engaged not only in the religious occasions but also in the day-to-day events in the lives of our friends, the middle-class parishioners of Most Holy Name.

The School

A huge boost to the already immensely popular pastoral work going on at Most Holy Name came when we opened two grades of the parochial school just a year after the parish began. Especially the parents with small children applauded this new service their parish now offered. The school was a most welcome extension of what was going on at Most Holy Name and further evidence that the American Franciscans were both serious about our commitment and capable of moving forward quickly with such a significant undertaking as the parish school.

From the first day the children were expected to arrive on time each morning with their school uniforms in perfect order. The beginning two grades held about twenty-five to thirty boys and girls each, and the recently completed classrooms received a thorough cleaning each afternoon by a few domestic workers now employed by the parish. Most Holy Name School copied the American-style parochial school system to the letter, and it was just what the middle-class parents had hoped their new parish would provide. The school was to be self-supporting, which meant that only those who could pay the tuition necessary for maintaining it and providing the funds for its continued expansion got to enroll their children.

To cover the first several months of that initial school year, I contracted with a small group of skilled Peruvian lay teachers to run the school. Meanwhile, backed by my New York Franciscan province, I negotiated successfully with the Sisters Servants of the Immaculate Heart of Mary with headquarters in Scranton, Pennsylvania, for sisters to staff this new initiative. Four of their members arrived in Lima as the school was completing its first three months and I immediately put them in charge of its entire administration. (This was more of an admission on my part that I had no expertise whatsoever in education or the management of a school than it was a magnanimous gesture of delegation.) The sisters began their work immediately and together with the original lay teachers quickly made the school a top-notch educational center.

One small philosophical impasse arose between the school parents and me as the school took shape. It hardly presaged what would later occur, but served to show that differences of outlook regarding the role of the school could well arise. With the presence of North American sisters in several of the classrooms, the parents wanted the school to function solely in English. These sophisticated middle- and upper-middle-class families knew that a command of English would prove a decided, long-term advantage for their children. Therefore they urged us to immerse their boys and girls from first grade on in the language which would be increasingly useful, even necessary, in the cosmopolitan world the children would one day enter. Though I had no background in pedagogy, I sensed instinctively that an all-English-speaking school was not a very good idea. It seemed that many cultural, historic and even spiritual values would be sacrificed to such a pragmatic educational approach. After consulting with a Peruvian child psychologist who backed up this gut feeling I'd had, I felt confident enough to insist that classes would be taught in Spanish, with English as a decidedly minor subject. The parents were not happy with my decision but went along with it, mainly because of the quality of education their children were getting in Most Holy Name School.

Outreach to the Poor

Despite our concentration on the middle and upper middle class, some outreach to the other two groups of parishioners—the domestic workers and the caretakers—did happen in these early years. Looking back on those efforts it would have to be said that they were superficial, token gestures, which demonstrated that we Franciscans really did not know how to serve the poor. At best these little outreach programs satisfied some of the demands of basic charity and they at least acknowledged the presence in the parish of others besides the well-off middle-class people. However, we completely overlooked any of the underlying causes for the second-class status of these poor parishioners of ours—we didn't have any preparation for that sort of analysis. Later we would be forced to remedy this blind spot.

We invited the domestic workers to the parish house about once every month for weekday afternoon social and religious gatherings. For a couple of hours the young servants would share some food, perhaps play a game or two and usually receive a short talk on some aspect of faith from one of the middle-class wives. However, I don't remember any serious effort to converse one-on-one with these young people, much less any inquiry about their lives in the homes of the well-to-do—for example, their wages, the treatment they received at the hands of their employers or "privileges" such as vacations, days off, or schooling. Nevertheless, these get-togethers were popular with the domestic workers, as they provided a safe, relaxing environment and a break from the boring routine of their lives. For many months the afternoon gatherings flourished, attendance increased and some recognition and familiarity grew between the young workers and the Franciscans at the parish.

The domestic workers for the most part attended the early Mass on Sunday mornings, sent by the homeowners who felt that as "good Catholics" they should at least allow time for the employees to fulfill their Sunday obligation. I never thought much about the matter then, but it really would have been more beneficial had the domestics observed those Sabbath days of rest by getting an extra hour of sleep. Later this early Mass would serve as a wonderful opportunity for serious catechesis and social analysis. But in these first years attending the Eucharist was more or less a routine and obligatory exercise for the domestics, and we Franciscans had no clue about how to offer a gospel message which would touch their lives. The servants came to Mass dressed in their work clothes and hurried back to their houses as soon as the service ended. They were always fearful of annoying the middle-class families who expected the domestics to wait on them as they lazed through their own leisurely Sunday mornings.

In these beginning years the caretakers got even less personal attention than the domestics did from us at Most Holy Name Parish. An essentially "invisible" population, transient in the extreme and, typically, passive and undemanding—in part because they were almost entirely consumed with the daily struggle for survival—the watchmen and their families had little contact with the parish. Sunday mornings found them too tired, or perhaps too embarrassed, to attend Mass. Simply put, there was really nothing for these marginalized folk at the middle-class liturgies celebrated at Most Holy Name. The caretakers would have felt embarrassed and out of place at Mass with the wealthy members of the parish; furthermore, there was no message in our preaching that had much relevance for this unfortunate segment of the population. What contact they did have with the parish nearly always took the form of begging for some favor or the occasional request for a baptism, usually of a sick child.

Nevertheless, we did try. It was clear from the house visits around the parish, which inevitably took us to the construction sites and the shacks of the caretakers, that the general health of this population was very poor. In addition, these needy people themselves often approached the parish in search of help with their various ailments. Indeed, one of the findings of the sociological study of the parish mentioned above was that the caretakers knew the parish to be a place where their needs would be taken seriously. We did pretty well with these charitable tasks.

To do something about the medical problems of the caretakers, I sought the services of two parishioners who were doctors and we began a small first aid station in the basement of the parish auditorium. This *posta médica*, as it was called, functioned for a few hours each afternoon and helped the caretaker families receive a modicum of treatment for their constant problems. When an urgent case presented itself, the doctors at the *posta* would refer the person to a local clinic or hospital. Often one of us Franciscans would get a call from the *posta* to drive a desperately sick person to an emergency room, where our presence might serve as "encouragement" for the admitting personnel to treat the person, since poor people could just as easily be turned away from any given medical facility.

It didn't always work. On one occasion I arrived at a private hospital with a dying baby and her mother, only to be told by the doctor on duty at the emergency room that the Children's Hospital would better serve the little one. Without thinking, in my haste to get help for the baby, I rushed her and her mother back to the car and set out for the Children's Hospital. On the way the child died. As I realized what had happened I turned around and went back to confront the doctor who had sent us off, threatening a malpractice lawsuit. (In the end I did not follow through on my threat, since the time and expense involved would be so much more than a poor family could afford, and could well prove unsuccessful in the end. We did manage to scare the doctor, I later found out. He wasn't sure that the American priest would not carry out the lawsuit.)

Another small outreach program for the caretakers was the afternoon classes we began to offer to their children in the school classrooms after the rich little kids had finished their day. Young high school or college age volunteers spent a couple of hours each day offering basic courses in reading and writing to the poor children. Again, in hindsight, this effort was tokenism, no doubt assuaging the consciences of all of us connected with our elitist day school. Perhaps for that reason the little afternoon school (*escuelita*, as it was called), like the medical post, was hailed as an example of the wonderful "social consciousness" present in Most Holy Name. (The parish was gaining a reputation on all fronts.) But like the medical post, the *escuelita* really served as an example of addressing symptoms rather than causes.

We also inaugurated Christmas bazaars for the domestic workers and the caretakers. At first these took the form of traditional handouts of used clothes and toys collected from the wealthy parishioners, gestures which made us middle-class folks feel good. One Christmas Eve I took a large bag of such handouts to the shack of one caretaker family and as I walked away, I heard the delighted cry of a little boy who had found *mi carrito* (a toy car for him) inside the bag. That little encounter served as one of those "human interest" stories which comfortable people find so soothing in Christmas homilies. Again, however, this give-away Christmas program was paternalistic and further dehumanizing to its passive recipients.

Soon after, we made this practice into a two-day rummage sale in the large basement of the parish auditorium. The donated clothes and toys were displayed on tables around the large room and the poor families came in to select what they wished as Christmas presents for their families, paying nominal prices for these goods. There always seemed to be enough donated goods to satisfy everyone. While it was still charity without social analysis, the bazaar proved to be one of the initiatives which lasted through all of the fundamental changes which would eventually come at Most Holy Name. It was an instant and genuine success in which everyone profited. The poor picked out and paid for the gifts which they themselves wished to give, rather than being on the receiving end of someone else's selection. And we let them know that the money they spent at the bazaar would be ploughed right back into the *posta médica* for medicines.

A "Martyr" for the Parish

On a Sunday afternoon in the summer of 1966 one of the Franciscans who had joined me at Most Holy Name, a dedicated and popular lay brother, Anselm Donohue, drowned while swimming at a beach not far from the parish. Anselm loved the ocean and body surfing but on that fateful day he got caught in a strong undertow so common along Peru's Pacific shore and really never had a chance. His body was rescued by two young men, who braved the ocean's pull and dragged Anselm to shore. It was a sudden and devastating loss for our Franciscan community as well as for the parish. His wake and funeral (the Franciscans have the custom of burying our deceased missionaries in the place where they are serving) produced an outpouring of love and concern on the part of the parishioners for all of us North American religious, and led to even greater bonds of unity in the parish. In Anselm's memory the soon-to-be-completed parish auditorium bore his name. The young parish now had a martyr.

The reaction of the cardinal to Anselm's death at the beach reflected what was said previously in this chapter about the image of religious as some sort of withdrawn "cloister dwellers" in the minds of many Peruvians. His Eminence called me to offer his condolences on our loss and to inquire about arrangements for the funeral. In the course of our conversation the cardinal urged me to play down as much as possible the fact that Anselm drowned while swimming at a public beach, as if there were something improper about it.

A Parish Council

During a 1966 furlough in the United States, I had the opportunity to reflect on some of the renewal that was just beginning to make itself felt after the recently completed (1965) Second Vatican Council. I found it interesting that the church in the United States put its emphasis on very different aspects of Pope John's *aggiornamento* ("dawn" or modernization) than what I was seeing in Peru and elsewhere in Latin America. For example, in the States there seemed to be intense discussion and considerable conflict over the many liturgical reforms coming into use. People in the U.S. were having these great battles, tempests in teapots to my way of thinking, over Mass in the vernacular, altars facing the people, and Eucharist in the form of wine as well as bread. In Latin America these changes were taking place much more smoothly, and without all the pushing and pulling up north—a tribute, I thought, to the Latino tendency not to worry about the small stuff. As it turned out, this easy acceptance of what turned out to be essentially cosmetic changes in church life proved fortunate for Latin America, which would have division enough of its own when the Second Vatican Council made its impact at the Medellín Conference of 1968.

I returned to the parish from my couple of months in the United States with the idea of implementing at Most Holy Name one of the outgrowths of the Council's emphasis on the place of the laity in church life, the parish council. This decision proved to be a very important step in setting a future course for the parish. The idea of the parish council, as I had come to know it in the States, was still imbedded in the old model of church. The pastor would gather parishioners who had expertise in the various "secular" aspects of administration—finances and construction for example—and employ them as a board of advisors, a kind of administrative cabinet. Ultimate authority stayed with the pastor. Initially, the parish council at Most Holy Name followed the top-down advisory style—pastor to parishioners—a model which everyone still accepted. In fact the Spanish name, *consejo parroquial* (parish advisory board), connoted something of my original intent for the group.

I went ahead and hand-picked the best parishioners I knew from the various professions and businesses, and invited them to serve as consultants in the administration of Most Holy Name. For their part, these designees were only too glad to lend their expertise to the ongoing physical development and management of the parish. They were, after all, part of the large majority of parishioners who had come to feel a sense of pride in the new experience of church that was Most Holy Name.

By sheer luck, one decision which I did not make as the parish council took shape gave this body the space to exercise a defining role in the parish as time went on. We never went down the road of by-laws or rules of procedure for the council, a non-decision which left that body free to become what it needed to be in the life of the parish. Only later did I see this open-ended management style as right in line with the much-favored mode of operation in the Latin American way of doing things. A favorite saying among the Latinos, "To make the road by walking it," was the way they described their preferred way of organizing. And we more or less fell into this by beginning our parish council with hardly any rules and regulations. In contrast we heard about another parish with the same social makeup as Most Holy Name but pastored by perhaps somewhat more organized (i.e., controlling) priests, whose parish council found itself so bound by its own rules about procedure, voting and decision-making that in effect it became an entity unto itself, pretty much separated from the life of the parish. It was like a well-functioning machine that had no practical purpose.

Under this free style of conducting the parish council's business, my original concept of the group as simply an advisory board quickly and (I suspect) inevitably developed into something much more significant and effective. The people I selected for the first parish council (all from the ranks of the homeowners, of course) knew infinitely more about their people, their history, culture and religious traditions than we foreigners did. In addition, as educated and well-informed women and men, they had kept up with what was taking place in the church in the wake of the now-completed Second Vatican Council. It was only a matter of a short time, then, before they expanded their role as my advisors in areas of their professional competence to include matters central to the life of the parish. I don't remember any debate or decision around this shift. It just seemed to fall into place naturally. We Franciscans saw the logic and value of such an arrangement and actively promoted this new and innovative equation between laity, religious and clergy.

In a short time, then, the parish council became the think tank for

Most Holy Name. It set out appropriate pastoral goals and objectives for the parish, designed the themes for Sunday liturgies, especially in particular seasons such as Advent and Lent, and generally established and directed what came to be called the *línea*—thrust, approach, orientation—for the entire parish project. The council met at least monthly to discuss the *línea*, to look at how we were implementing it (by critiquing our homilies, for example) and to review the results among the parishioners. Once each year the parish council devoted an entire weekend to updating and adjusting various aspects of the *línea*, especially as the wider church in Latin America incorporated the Second Vatican Council into its life. Administrative matters still came in for discussion at council meetings, but the scope of its vision and purpose became ever wider.

Looking back on this remarkable experience of a parish council which took on both the administrative and the visioning tasks of the parish, I often wonder how we managed to do it, especially when the calls for radical social change began to come from the larger church. After all, the members of the council came from the same privileged group of parishioners (we were never able to incorporate representatives of the other sectors of the parish, due mainly to the vast social gap between these and the middle-class members). Still, they caught the spirit which was driving the Latin American church at that time, and showed a great willingness to see it implemented in the parish. Through annual elections to the parish council we renewed its membership by a third every year and with very few exceptions the new members also accepted and promoted the changes taking place. How did such unanimity come about?

One reason for this success story, I believe, had to do with the vision of church, the mystique if you will, which unified the parish council. While I never remember seeing it in writing, except at the very end of my time at Most Holy Name when a new group of North American Franciscans came to take over, the council had constantly in mind a common vision of what church ought to be. New members quickly made the vision their own—almost, it seemed, by osmosis. Another reason for our unified outlook was the annual review weekends, mentioned above, which the parish council engaged in at the beginning of each year.

There all of us had the opportunity to ask any questions we wanted about where the parish was going and how it could best get there. The *línea* was constantly refined and adjusted, and all of the parish council members bought into it. I've always thought, too, that we enjoyed a special blessing of the Holy Spirit during those years, especially with regard to the experience of the parish council. The "new Pentecost" which Pope John XXIII had predicted as he began the Second Vatican Council, and which the bishops of Latin America had continued to experience as they applied the Council to their world, surely influenced the church at local levels. I often marveled at the insights and decisions which our parish council arrived at in those years. They could only have been the work of the Holy Spirit.

In this new context of the parish council as the defining body for Most Holy Name, all of us Franciscans moved from positions of near-absolute clerical authority to more collegial, collaborative, democratic roles. We saw ourselves as members of the council, sharing as equals in its discussions and decisions. In fact, as time went on and this unique arrangement became the norm at Most Holy Name, with the parish council members growing more comfortable and more public in their position as the parish's servant leaders, and with the *línea* becoming ever more prophetic and challenging, the cardinal began to get nervous about the situation. On at least one occasion he asked me who had the final say in the decision-making processes of the parish. I consistently dodged the question, knowing that I could not give the answer His Eminence wanted—that I as pastor had the ultimate say in parish matters—because it simply was not true. Instead, I continually countered the Archbishop's question by telling him that we never dealt with "ultimate questions" in the parish council. Our concern centered on pastoral, practical questions—how best to preach the gospel and implement church teaching in the social context of Most Holy Name. My evasion always irritated His Eminence and this tension between us continued for the rest of my years in the parish.

There were a few times when the parish council at Most Holy Name proposed initiatives I did not entirely agree with. One such discussion had to do with the need for a yearly parish fair and fundraiser, called *kermeses* in Lima—a custom in middle-class parishes of the Lima Archdiocese, which produced tens of thousands of dollars but which involved immense expenditures of time and energy. From the beginning I had avoided *kermeses* as too time-consuming for the parish staff and volunteers, and had written them off as essentially gimmicks to raise money, which to my way of thinking should be coming from the comfortable middle-class parishioners anyway.

However, as the start-up money from the New York Franciscans for Most Holy Name Parish began to dry up and more responsibility for its financial health rested on the parishioners, the parish council began to make noises in favor of starting *kermeses*. As a member of the council, I argued against the idea, pointing out that such a departure would change the entire course of parish finances and ministries. Once we began to depend on the *kermeses* we would be hooked, spending a lot of time each year preparing for the next *kermés* or getting over the last one. But I also let the other members of the council know that I would hold to my word and go along with the majority opinion should they decide in favor of the policy change.

In the end, whether because of my acknowledged place as the "founding pastor," or due to the persuasiveness of the argument against the change, or simply the better judgment of others on the parish council, a different, more direct method for raising money was chosen. The debate and decision, nevertheless, marked a decisive moment in the evolution of the parish council. Both the seriousness of the issue and my own role as simply one more voting member of the council demonstrated to the others on the board that they all exercised true leadership in the parish, even in cases where I disagreed with them. The parish council never wavered thereafter in assuming responsible and sometimes unpopular leadership at Most Holy Name.

Cursillo *Movement*

One initiative that helped us solidify the Parish Council was our engagement with the *Cursillo* (literally "short course") Movement, which appeared in Lima during those early post-Vatican II years. A kind of Catholic revival, which had recently originated in Spain, the *Cursillo* featured intense weekend retreats for laymen and women. From Friday evening until Sunday afternoon the participants were subjected to a series of almost non-stop, marathon conferences on Catholic faith and morals and a very emotional renewal of the sacramental practices. The priest who arrived in Peru to initiate this Movement was an energetic and quite effective young Spaniard, who achieved immediate success among the kind of middle-class people who made up Most Holy Name Parish.

For a year or two in the mid-60s many of our parishioners became *cursillistas* and, as mentioned, gave us a cadre of newly inspired Catholic laity for our Parish Council's growing role as the defining body at Most Holy Name. However, despite my initial enthusiasm for and promotion of the *Cursillo* among the parishioners, I quickly became disillusioned over what I considered strong-arm methods used on the more "recalcitrant" (thoughtful) participants in these weekend sessions, particularly with regard to insistence on Confession and the reception of the Eucharist. I felt that at times people's consciences were violated by the team of presenters, including and especially the Spanish priest himself and I quietly disassociated myself from the movement. (As a matter of fact the Archdiocese of Lima formally disbanded the activities of the *Cursillo* some time later for its divisiveness.)

Nevertheless, for a time the reinvigoration of personal faith and practice, which the *Cursillo* brought to members of Most Holy Name, did serve to bolster our Parish Council. Looking back on that experience, it is clear that the *Cursillo* represented a serious attempt to energize the laity. However, its questionable methods and its concentration on individual piety without any social analysis made the movement ultimately an anachronism for us.

Honeymoon Years

Thus our young parish moved through its beginning years. Even beyond the limits of Most Holy Name we were making a name for ourselves. People moving into the parish heard beforehand of the updated, people-oriented pastoral approaches at Most Holy Name, as well as the progressive attitudes of the "cool" American Franciscans in charge there. The parish house, classrooms for the first several grades of the school and a large parish auditorium provided an adequate infrastructure for the ever-growing numbers of newcomers. The open and inclusive understanding of sacramental life on the part of our pastoral team at Most Holy Name symbolized all the other activities going on in the parish. Thanks to the parish council and its cultural influence on us Americans, the pastoral style at Most Holy Name became increasingly congenial to the Peruvian mentality. The parish school, headed by competent American sisters, and adding a new grade level each year, continued its success story as an important dimension of the overall thrust of Most Holy Name. My daily visits and those of the other Franciscans to parishioners' homes led to a growing sense of unity among the people as well as increasing attendance at Mass and the other sacraments. The parish-sponsored fiestas in the parish house, or some similar upscale venue in line with the tastes of the upper middle class, and our participation in family birthdays, wedding receptions and other social events rounded out an image of Holy Name Parish as a great place to belong.

These several and in many ways astute pastoral steps in the early life of Most Holy Name Parish produced what was truly a "honeymoon" period. The Franciscans and the Sisters had gained the good will of just about everybody in the parish as well as people outside who were observing the progress of this new church phenomenon. Our successful, if unexamined, concentration on the privileged sector of the parish resulted in favorable reports about Most Holy Name beyond its boundaries. Even the leaders of the Franciscan province in New York heard, to their delight, of the "great" things that were going on in the new Peruvian mission. On an official visit to Most Holy Name in those early years one of our Franciscan superiors from the United States jokingly expressed doubts about whether the Holy Spirit was truly behind the efforts there, since everything was proceeding so smoothly (the inference being that God tests all beginnings with adversity and there seemed to be none at Most Holy Name).

In hindsight, these happy years and the growing reputation of Most Holy Name served a lasting purpose. Together with a small handful of similarly oriented (generally American-run) parishes, it held out to Peruvian Catholics an attractive view of church, of religion, of clergy and religious and of parish life itself, after centuries of what one might caricature as "Spanish" or "European" rigidity. In addition, the honeymoon period would stand the parish in good stead as events moved toward the dynamic application of Second Vatican Council to the Latin American social and religious reality—the 1968 Medellín Conference. In its first four years Most Holy Name Parish built up a fund of good will among its members, which would see them through the revision and consequent changes, misunderstandings and conflicts that awaited them.

Personally, I could not have been happier with the way things were going. One event which took place just as the parish marked its third anniversary seemed to symbolize many of the things we had accomplished thus far. A prosperous businessman in the parish had come down with a fatal blood disease. During his subsequent lengthy stays in the hospital or periods of convalescence at home one of us visited him daily, so that we came to know him and his family very well. At the end of 1966 it was clear that he had only a short time to live and he asked to be taken home from the hospital for one last New Year's Eve party, to which he invited a few close friends. We Franciscans and the Sisters were among the small group that gathered to celebrate with the dying man and his family in their lovely home. It was a typical upper-middle-class fiesta, complete with free-flowing drinks, abundant food and congenial company. The host made us forget his desperate situation as he entertained us with funny stories, got us all singing and at midnight toasted the New Year with us. Four days later we celebrated his funeral. On reflection, all of us Americans agreed that this remarkable experience in a way summarized everything we wished for our ministry—good pastoral attention and engagement with our parishioners especially at the peak moments of their lives.

Soon enough we would understand how very limited our vision had been!

CHAPTER 4

A Turning Point

Red Flags

Within this near textbook-perfect process of building a new parish, several warning flags went up as Most Holy Name moved into its fourth year. One was raised as the result of a visit I got from a delegation of parishioners, all men, who came with the idea of constructing a social club on parish property—the funding for which, in their plan, I would secure. In the minds of these sharp professionals the idea had a lot of merit. There was no such center in the vicinity, so obviously, they said, the need was there. In addition, they told me, a club would serve to help along my efforts to unite the community socially as well as religiously. As for the funding, well, I had burst upon the scene just a couple of years before and in record time—with large amounts of money that I seemed able to draw freely from my New York province—had overseen the construction of a fairly complete parish plant. Surely, these parishioners thought, there was more money where those funds had come from. Besides, as they pointed out correctly, thanks to the original donation from the fabulously wealthy Castañeda family, Most Holy Name had enough land to accommodate such a social center.

We never did get to the specifics of the proposal: who would design the building and oversee its construction and administration; would it be exclusively a men's club, a possibility which obviously had its own problems; was the money I would get going to be a loan or an outright donation? I immediately understood that these comfortable middle-class professionals wanted a place of leisure which catered to their already highly developed tastes—a posh environment, perhaps with an adjacent swimming pool. Who knew how far their dreams had taken them? However, the conversation never progressed that far. For I quickly took a very different view of their proposal. My reaction was critical to the point of sarcasm: did they think that I and the other Franciscans had come to Peru in order to finance and build social clubs for the privileged? Did they see the parish as a kind of sinecure for them and their comfortable peers? I remember even going so far as to tell them that up until that moment I had considered them fairly intelligent people but now I was not so sure. The project, needless to say, never saw the light of day. The experience taught me that my middle-class parishioners were capable of viewing us Franciscans and the parish in a very different light from the way we saw ourselves and our mission.

A more ominous red flag appeared with respect to the afternoon gatherings of domestic workers. I began to notice that attendance at these biweekly recreational and catechetical events had fallen off noticeably and I asked one of the middle-class women who often helped out with their organization about the drop-off. With uncharacteristic bluntness, she told me that during their hours together at the parish house the domestics had taken to comparing notes with one another about such matters as salaries, working conditions in their respective households, opportunities for schooling and vacations. "We believe that they are becoming spoiled," the woman said, and for that reason many of the middle-class employers were feeling that it would be better not to allow their servants time off for these parish activities. In my mind the obvious question arose: how did this situation fit with the image of the progressive parish community at Most Holy Name of which everyone was so proud? Were we really what we seemed to be?

Another less immediate but no less powerful signal that all might not be entirely well at Most Holy Name came from an unexpected source. In March of 1967 Pope Paul VI issued his historic encyclical, "On the Development of Peoples." The papal statement analyzed the situation of the haves and the have-nots in the world and called for serious attention to the growing gap between the two. The document dealt with global realities, of course, but to us at Most Holy

Name Parish, Pope Paul's words felt enormously relevant. Here we had a numerical minority of middle- and upper-middle-class Peruvians (together with us equally middle-class North American priests and religious)—the haves—sitting atop a pyramid of increasing poverty represented by the domestic workers and the caretaker families—the have-nots—and all part of the one parish. Indeed, I reflected, the parish presented a mirror image of the global reality described in the Pope's encyclical of relatively few people hoarding God-given benefits meant for all people. Where was the equity, where was the fairness, where was the justice in the faith community of Most Holy Name Parish? Wasn't this papal statement clearly about us?

The relevance and challenge of the Pope's encyclical struck home directly after a Saturday evening Mass late in 1967. On the steps of the auditorium a member of the parish, a man engaged in national politics and generally outspoken on any number of subjects, publicly criticized me about the homily I had just given, in which I had quoted extensively from the Pope's encyclical. The man's objection to what I had said was that it was Marxist thinking, and when I suggested that I had merely followed the line of reasoning outlined in Pope Paul's letter, the bombastic parishioner said that yes, the pontiff tended toward communism, too. Since the parishioner was a public figure, the incident got reported in the newspapers and on TV. It was becoming clear to me that on various levels and in a number of ways certain lines in the sand were beginning to be drawn in Most Holy Name Parish, lines which could take us to God knew where.

Now, at a distance of three decades, I try to recall how these different signals of changes in the air affected my thinking at that time about all that had been accomplished at Most Holy Name and where we were headed. I don't remember any of these incidents in particular causing serious rethinking on my part. However, this fourth year at Most Holy Name proved to be a turning point. The change that was happening was organic and therefore gradual (perhaps a good sign that it was valid). What is clear is the fact that at the end of 1967 our thinking had come a distance from where it had been when we toasted the New Year in the comfortable home of a dying businessman twelve months before. We Franciscans and the parish council now had many questions about this "successful" parochial enterprise we had created.

Medellín

Just as these warning signals appeared in Most Holy Name, a historic, Spirit-led event took place in the Latin American Catholic world which gave us a lens through which to look at what was happening in the parish. It would be impossible to overstate the impact which the August 1968 Second General Conference of Latin American Bishops made on every dimension of the church and society in Latin America. I write about the Conference in some detail here because as an ordinary parish priest I experienced the powerful effect it had on all of us who were working at local levels of church life. This remarkable gathering and its aftermath was like some great avalanche of breakthrough thinking and prophetic statements that rolled over us and left us stunned by its power. I would have to say that even more than Vatican Council II itself, this Conference affected my life and ministry, my understanding of the gospel and life in God, affected me to the core of my being.

This meeting became known as the Medellín Conference, after the city in Colombia where it was held. It brought together representatives from the bishops' conferences of South and Central America and the Caribbean to apply to their part of the world all of the remarkable insights and innovations that had recently come out of the Second Vatican Council. Thanks to its courageous and truly visionary architects, among them Peruvians Cardinal Juan Landazuri (the man who had invited us Franciscans to undertake the new parish) and theologian Father Gustavo Gutiérrez, the Medellín Conference succeeded beyond anyone's expectations. As I said, it has to be seen as a movement of the Holy Spirit—much like Vatican II itself—one which shook both the church and society throughout Latin America and far beyond to their foundations.

No other local, national or continental church felt the effects of the Council during the late 1960s and into the 1970s as did Latin America, thanks to Medellín. While Vatican II proved a watershed event across the entire Catholic world, I have a feeling that in many places (like the United States) its effects remained on a superficial, even cosmetic level for many years. In this I stand open to correction, because after all I did not live the post-Vatican II years anywhere but in Latin America. But as we began to experience the profound effects of the Medellín Conference and its application of the Council to our church life, for a decade or more it seemed to me that the Catholic Church in other countries and on other continents did not take the Council as seriously or apply it as profoundly as did the church in the southern half of the Americas. In Peru, for example, we were hearing reports of debates at every level of the church in the United States around questions like receiving Communion in the hand rather than on the tongue. In Latin America these were simply non-issues. Rather, the Medellín Conference, enlightened by the Second Vatican Council, went to the very heart of what it means to be church, communities of faith, the People of God. The genius of the Latin American bishops in calling for that continent-wide congress to debate the Council's breakthrough insights seemed to me to have made all the difference. To my mind the Latin American church at Medellín wrestled with exactly the right questions about how best to live out the vision of the great conciliar document "The Church in the Modern World." I believe that sort of broad-gauged, all-inclusive application of Vatican II only gradually—and some would say inconclusively—happened in the churches of North America, Asia and Africa.

At Medellín, in a series of short documents, the predominant realities of Latin American life were summarized, subjected to a social analysis, and then considered in the light of the gospel. Among these were family and demography, youth, education, lay movements, mass media, peace and justice. Each document ended with a call for pastoral action, often urging totally new ways of dealing with the reality under discussion. For example, in the document on youth the bishops subtly turned the church's previous authoritarian approach to young people on its head. "[The youth] expect pastors not only to preach doctrinal principles but to back them up by concrete attitudes and actions. . . . [Therefore] . . . the Church in Latin America should be manifested, in an increasingly clear manner, as truly poor, missionary and paschal, separate from all temporal power and courageously committed to the liberation of each and every man [sic]." On practically every page of the Medellín documents the Conference looked at the most obvious question facing Latin America, the overriding poverty in which the majority of the Latin Americans live. They called this situation "institutionalized violence" and declared that it was the deadly combination of wealthy Latin American interests intertwined with oppressive international economic institutions which had brought about and held in place the impoverishment of the entire continent. The bishops called for every effort on the part of pastoral workers to help overthrow this oppressive and scandalous situation: "The Church . . . will lend its support to the downtrodden of every social class so that they might come to know their rights and how to make use of them." The Medellín Conference also honestly acknowledged the complicity of the church itself in this toxic mix of national and international vested interests and called for its famous "preferential option for the poor" at every level of church life—from grassroots lay catechists through the mid-level parish workers, right up to the hierarchy itself.

A simple listing of the issue areas addressed by the bishops and theologians at Medellín shows a broad-gauged, deep examination of conscience which the Conference made for the whole Latin American church. Under the rubric of "human promotion" the participants took up the issues of justice, peace, family and demography, education and youth; under "evangelization and growth in the faith" they looked at pastoral care for the masses, catechesis and liturgy. Looking at the "visible church and its structures," they addressed issues concerning lay movements, priests, religious, formation of the clergy, poverty of the church, joint pastoral planning and mass media. No area of church or secular life remained unexamined at Medellín.

Of particular interest to all of us at Most Holy Name was one particular document entitled "Pastoral Concern for the Elites." After defining what it means by "elites"—professionals, political and military leaders, artists, professors, etc.—the document goes on to lay out and analyze the differing mindsets among these groups. Of note for Most Holy Name was the critique in this particular document of the "traditionalists" or "conservatives," many of whom were found in our parish. "In general," said the document, "they are primarily concerned with preserving their privileges, which they identify with the 'established order.' Their community action takes the character of paternalism and almsgiving, with no concern for changing the status quo." This was a snapshot of Most Holy Name Parish, and we studied it carefully.

For me and many pastoral workers, one particularly important aspect of the Medellín Conference was the methodology alluded to above. Rejecting the traditional "top down" process which so many of us had been taught, wherein religious and ethical principles are applied uniformly to practical issues and circumstances, the bishops and theologians at Medellín began with Latin America's real-life issues and their causes, and offered the gospel and pastoral insights coming from these analyses. It was a "bottom up" approach, from practice to theory.

As we shall see, this methodology coincided with that of liberation theology, which was just then appearing on the horizon in the Latin American church. In applying the Scriptures to their economic, cultural, sociological and ecclesiastical world, the participants at Medellín followed the example of Pope Paul VI, who, in the encyclical, "On the Development of People," used the same methodology. When he spoke of the desperate poverty which cripples so many human beings today, the Pope said: "It is a question . . . of building a world where every man, no matter what his race, religion or nationality, can live a fully human life, freed from servitude imposed on him by other men or by natural forces over which he has not sufficient control; a world where freedom is not an empty word and [note the Scriptural application] *where the poor man Lazarus can sit down at the same table with the rich man*" (No. 47). The process moved from the real circumstances of life to the reflection on God's Word which those circumstances sparked. This "bottom up" approach gave us at Most Holy Name a way to carry on continuous dialogue among ourselves about what was happening in our world and how we needed to respond.

Because of the central role of Lima's Cardinal Landazuri and theologian Gustavo Gutiérrez in that consensus-shattering conference, we in the Peruvian church immediately felt its impact. Within weeks of its conclusion we were receiving classes on the many pastoral implications of Medellín from the very people who had articulated them. Quickly, the effects of Medellín spread across the entire Latin American church and society. Laity, religious, priests, theologians and bishops, who for years had found themselves unsure about how to confront the scandalous chasm between the lives of grinding poverty lived by the majority of their people and the extravagant wealth and power enjoyed by elites both inside and outside Latin America, now had guidelines for action.

Situations across Latin America, where political and military power combined with economic and religious underpinnings to hold in place the unjust status quo, led pastoral workers under the guidance of the Medellín documents to raise their voices and call for reactions from their people. When the Conference called the injustices of their societies "institutionalized violence," people understood it as a challenge to do something about this evil. I believe we can point to this moment of grace in the Latin American church and society as the beginning of many subsequent struggles for liberation that took place as the decade of the 1960s ended and the 1970s began. These were responses, direct and indirect, to the Medellín Conference's call for fundamental structural change which Medellín set forth. It was a revolutionary moment in the best sense of the word—a turning over of unjust structures, of the institutionalized sin, which oppressed people across the length and breadth of Latin America.

For us who were only beginning to ask hard questions about the Latin American status quo, Medellín offered a methodology and insights on how to think about the world we were part of and take some beginning steps in response. To my mind, one of the great teachings of the Medellín Conference (and of liberation theology and conscientization as well) was the insistence that the injustice done to the majority of the people in Latin America together with all of its dehumanizing consequences were not only economic or political or sociological problems but gospel ones as well. They are, therefore, pastoral questions too. It was a lesson I never forgot.

Two other phenomena helped us enormously in this gospel revolution—the rise of liberation theology and the development of Paulo Freire's process of "conscientization." Coming as they did just about the same time as Medellín, these tools of analysis and action became pathways for putting into practice the vision that conference had set forth. Liberation theology and conscientization put flesh and bones on the radically new pastoral approaches held out to us by Medellín in so many places, not least of all in Most Holy Name Parish.

Liberation Theology

The new understanding of the poor in relation to the gospel of Jesus, which gradually took the name "liberation theology,"[1] grew out of the very heart and soul of Latin America, out of the lives of the oppressed and forgotten masses of women and men who live there. In their contact with the oppressed people of their countries, a number of serious and trained theologians such as Gustavo Gutiérrez in Peru, Segundo Galilea in Chile, Juan Luis Segundo in Uruguay and Jose Miguez Bonino in Argentina gradually came to see the intolerable lives being lived by the majority of the Latin American people as a questioning of the gospel itself.

Gutiérrez put it this way: "Does God's word have anything to say to 'non-human beings' " and went on to explain the startling phrase "non-human beings." It referred, he said, to the millions of women, children and men in Latin America who never have any chance at a life of even moderate dignity: the women, worn down early in life by malnutrition, multiple childbirths and the constant struggle for survival; the children, already undernourished at birth, who find themselves trapped in what Pope Paul VI described as the "vicious cycle of poverty" that is passed along from generation to generation; the men, denied education and meaningful job opportunities, living frustrated lives, eking out a "living" for themselves and their families through the most menial and unstable jobs. All "non-human beings."

The liberation theologians came to these insights because they did not operate in the ivory towers of academia. They put themselves in direct contact with the poor, living in the "barrios" and working in sprawling parishes which served them. The phrase the theologians used for this engagement with the poor spoke volumes about their intentions: *salir al encuentro*—literally, "going out to the encounter" (with the poor). I heard the story of a summertime visit by an upper-middle-class professor of law at Peru's Catholic University to Gustavo Gutiérrez's inner city apartment. Gutiérrez invited his distinguished guest inside and asked if he wished something to drink. When the professor answered that he would enjoy some refreshment on such a warm afternoon, Gustavo brought him a glass of water, the only drink available in the house: he had gone out to encounter the poor in a way the law professor had not previously imagined. The theologians also came to know the poor through frequent conversations with hundreds of church workers—priests, sisters, brothers and lay workers—who also lived and worked among the masses of poor people in Latin American cities and countryside. There was a great deal of sharing, based on enormous mutual respect, between pastors and theologians in those days. More will be said in chapter 6 on how the theologians solicited the experiences of local church workers.

The fundamental questioning of the gospel which sparked this new approach to theology raised the outrageous possibility that Jesus' message might only have relevance for the comfortable and the privileged of the world. That possibility seems absurd to us today. Everyone shares the good news of the gospel. But we have the advantage of Second Vatican Council, as well as the last forty years of Catholic social teaching, where concern about the plight of the poor stands at the center of Christian life. However, when the liberation theologians began asking this question, they were deadly serious. For years Christian preachers, theologians and catechists had accommodated the gospel and the Scriptures to the consciences of well-to-do Christians, perhaps especially in Latin America, thereby blunting the challenging messages of Jesus and the prophets. They placed emphasis, for example, on Saint Matthew's rendition of the Sermon on the Mount: "Blessed are you poor in spirit" (Matt. 5:3) and not on Saint Luke's stark phrase: "Blessed are you who are poor" (Luke 6:20). Under that cover even the most privileged segments of society could easily consider themselves "spiritually poor." "Life holds problems for everyone, and we are all needy," went the thinking.

What is more, the church in Latin America for centuries had helped keep the poor in their miserable place by preaching a gospel of "happiness in the hereafter." In this the church gave moral legitimacy to the dreadful status quo. The story was told of a prominent member of the Peruvian hierarchy who only a few years before had declared that a church with many poor among its members had God's blessing because it gave everyone else an opportunity to practice charity. In hindsight, such a statement clearly represents a betrayal of Christ's gospel, but at the time it reflected the thinking of a majority in the church and helped to maintain an unjust social organization which allowed very well-to-do people to live unconcerned lives alongside the impoverished masses. This awful imbalance was dismissed by more than one preacher as: "simply God's will." Liberation theology broke through such facile and impoverished thinking.

The answer to the question posed by the liberationist theologians—does God's Word have anything to say to non-human beings—held enormous consequences. For the answer pointed to a consistent, clear, even stern call from God for the liberation of the most needy: "I have heard the cry of my people. . . ." (Exodus 3:7); "This, rather, is the fasting that I wish: releasing those bound unjustly . . ." (Isaiah 58:6); "He has deposed the mighty from their thrones and raised the lowly to high places. . . ." (Luke 1:52); "I was hungry and you gave me to eat" (Matt. 25:35). The liberationists saw on virtually every page of the Bible judgments directed not only at individual situations of deprivation, but also at the structures of society which produced and sustained them—the "institutionalized violence" described by the Medellín documents which enveloped each and all poor persons.

As we came to know it, then, the theology of liberation was in no way the political program or agenda for social revolution that its critics have wished to categorize it as and thereby dismiss it. Rather, it was and continues to be a process by which every situation of oppression at any level of human life can be judged in the light of the Bible. It proved invaluable to all of us pastoral workers who felt called by Medellín to live out a "preferential option for the poor." When you think about it, this way of doing theology was not new at all. The gospels themselves came out of the lived experience and realities of the communities which gathered in Jesus' name. They represent a reflection on the life of Jesus as each community experienced it over a period of several decades. As will be seen, this new, or renewed, way of doing theology—theology as a reflection on reality in the light of God's word—profoundly influenced the thinking and action of all who were involved in pastoral work at Most Holy Name. It gave us a process for reflecting on our parish reality and of applying the teachings of the Medellín Conference to our work there.[2]

Conscientization
reflexive verb
evocative questions are key

The "conscientization" method, developed about this same time by the Brazilian educator, Paulo Freire, gave us pastoral people in Latin America a practical tool for implementing both the mandates of Medellín and the process of liberation theology. Freire had used literacy programs not only to teach reading and writing to peasants in Brazil, but also to raise their consciousness (for them to become conscientized) about the social content of the word they were learning. In Freire's system what he called "generative words," those which spark ideas, were learned and reflected on. Words like "house," "money," "food" in the conscientization method helped formerly illiterate peasants understand whole clusters of phrases which described concepts like fair and adequate housing, or wages that are insufficient for even a modest existence, or food which is both abundant and unavailable. This process led Freire's students to wide-ranging social analyses as they gradually became familiar with many of the social, economic and educational forces in societies like Brazil.

In its original Portuguese and later in Spanish "to conscientize" was a reflexive verb. That is, one did the process for oneself—no one "conscientized" another. Each person came to his or her own conclusions in learning and understanding these "generative words." For that reason, a guiding principle in Freire's method was absolute respect of teacher for student. No imposition of thought or analysis or conclusion was tolerated. Those who followed this rule helped produce independent-thinking and often self-starting communities of oppressed people.

Obviously this sort of growing awareness of their place in the world by marginalized people has enormous potential for social change. When poor and oppressed women and men open their eyes to the injustices being done to them, demands for a new order of things cannot be far off. Within a few years, therefore, the "Freireian method" became identified with revolution in the minds of powerful people in Brazil. Paulo Freire had to leave Brazil and later Chile when the reigning military governments of those countries saw his teaching methods stirring up the masses and becoming a threat to their positions of power.

This reasoning on the part of the establishment in Brazil and Chile was, of course, absolutely right. However, for so many people of faith in Latin America, especially those engaged in the pastoral directions pointed to by Medellín, the possibility of revolution which emerged from people becoming aware (conscientized) was simply a justified reaction to "institutionalized violence"—a modern version of God's demand of the Pharaoh in Egypt to "let my people go." The Medellín documents and the church's response to them would always call for nonviolent resistance and change to the extent possible in any revolutionary initiative. Nevertheless, it was clear that revolution in its root meaning—a turnaround of the existing situation—was what Medellín, liberation theology and Freire, in different ways, were calling for.

Thus, the Medellín guidelines, together with the processes of liberation theology and Paulo Freire's tools for conscientization, swept across Latin America in the late 1960s and the 1970s. At every level of church life the challenge to opt personally and institutionally for the poor, to place parishes, dioceses and schools, together with their personnel at the service of "the least of the sisters and brothers" played out in all sorts of creative ways. One striking example of this new way of being church came from the prestigious Society of Jesus. For centuries in Latin America the highly educated and influential Jesuits had dedicated themselves to the education of the privileged classes. Their rationale for this clear choice had seemed persuasive—give the elites a solid Christian formation and eventually society will change. The problem was that in practice the rationale had never worked. Nothing had changed. The chasm between the rich and the poor, between privilege and poverty remained in place year after year, decade after decade. Through the inspiration of Medellín, and with courageous leadership, especially on the part of Father Pedro Arrupe, their visionary Superior General at the time, the Jesuits set for themselves the goal of going out (*salir al encuentro*) of their fancy schools and closer to the underprivileged: living among them and offering them basic tools for living lives of dignity. They made personal and institutional options for the poor and set a powerful example for the whole church of Latin America. As Father Arrupe predicted, the Jesuits inevitably suffered enormously for their gospel choice.

The most dramatic example of what Father Arrupe prophesied happened in late 1989 when six Jesuit priests, together with two women who worked with them, met a brutal death at the University of Central America in El Salvador. The Jesuits there had turned the university into a model of institutionalized option for the poor at every level, something the Salvadoran army simply could not accept. So one November night a squad of killers broke into the Jesuit residence and systematically machine-gunned everyone in the house.

Medellín in Practice

In many areas of Central and South America the clarion call of Medellín to the whole church resulted in repressive, often violently repressive, measures from those with the most to lose—the wealthy and comfortable classes, backed by military power, which had benefited outrageously at the cost of the poor and marginalized. It was estimated that in the ten years which followed the Medellín Conference some eleven hundred church people—principally lay catechists, but also sisters, brothers, priests and even bishops—were killed in Latin America for attempting to implement this new way of being church. Often these murders happened to people who were doing nothing more revolutionary or subversive than accompanying the poor in parishes and doing other pastoral work.

For North Americans the most famous case of such "political killings" was that of the four American churchwomen brutalized and assassinated in December of 1980 in El Salvador. Transparent lies about these three religious and one lay women, painting them as active collaborators with the armed revolution in that country, backfired on the American politicians who told them. It became ever more clear that the women suffered martyrdom for the simple reason that they were sharing life with the poor of El Salvador whom they had come to love. That was their "crime."

As this "new Pentecost" dawned on the Latin American church, we at Most Holy Name Parish did not need much persuasion regarding the implementation of the Medellín guidelines for pastoral work. The now four-year-old parish was ripe for it. It was still in its beginning stages, without as yet the sort of entrenched customs ("we've always done it this way"), which can slow down or even make change impossible. As mentioned, the church of Lima, Peru, had contributed two of Medellín's principal architects, Cardinal Juan Landazuri and Father Gustavo Gutiérrez. Thanks to them the great Conference made its impact on all of us almost immediately. In addition the "red flags" which had appeared and made us ask some hard questions about the kind of parish community we were building among our parishioners fed right into the compelling message of Medellín. For all of us at Most Holy Name the guidelines set out at Medellín felt as though they had been written with our parish in mind.

Of immense importance, too, was the invitation I received to form part of a nation-wide priests' group which gathered around Gutiérrez and other Peruvian church leaders to deepen and further the insights and directives of Medellín. This opportunity proved to be another turning point for me personally, and for the parish I was serving.

Notes

[1] To be more accurate it is necessary to speak of liberation theologies (plural). In past years we have seen a variety of valid and insightful reflections on God's word coming out of different situations of oppression—that of women, of Afro-Americans, of Indigenous peoples. The phrase "liberation theology" in the context of this book refers to a new way of understanding the gospel based on the socioeconomic exclusion of the Latin American majorities. This is just one of many such theologies.

[2] In contrast to this analytical and fairly abstract description of liberation theology, I will describe in chapter 5 how I came into contact with liberation theology myself. Thanks to a great mentor, Gustavo Gutiérrez, this way of theologizing had everything to do with the parish I was serving and with the life of all of us who lived and worked there.

Prophetic as well as Pastoral

The invitation to join Father Gustavo Gutiérrez and his group was the result of a series of conferences which the parish council sponsored in May of 1968. The Medellín event was still a few months away, but its preparations were very much in progress and there were stirrings of its spirit among progressive church people in Latin America. In March of that year some leaders among the Peruvian clergy issued a detailed statement analyzing the social realities of their country and, as Medellín would soon do for all of Latin America, calling for conversion in their church and society. Nothing like this had ever happened before in Peru and the Cieneguilla document, named after the place where it was written, made headlines in the newspapers. It also sparked vigorous debate, especially among the better educated, who had always thought of their priests pretty much as sacramental bureaucrats and liked it that way. The priests' challenge to the status quo caused a number of these elites to advise them publicly to mind their own business. The parish council at Most Holy Name seized upon this unique circumstance and invited Gutiérrez together with two other signers of the statement to address the parish. The parishioners flocked to the sessions and debated the priests in wide-ranging and extremely contentious discussions.

An interesting footnote to this event came with the reaction from a member of the wealthy Castañeda family, who had formerly owned the entire area of the parish and had donated a large parcel of it for the parochial buildings. The matriarch of the family, a woman in her seventies, upon hearing that Father Gutiérrez and others of his group would be speaking in "her parish" (actually she did not live anywhere near Most Holy Name, but in the fashion of her aristocratic class she considered the family's former land holdings as still under their control), arrived some days before the conferences in her chauffeur-driven Mercedes to see me. She demanded that these radical and revolutionary priests not be allowed to set foot in the parish and when I said that we would go ahead with the planned conferences, Mrs. Castañeda took the matter to the cardinal. His Eminence knew he could not prevent talks from being given by priests who were among the best in his archdiocese, but he asked me at least to tone down the publicity surrounding the event. In the end, Mrs. Castañeda turned out to be a shrill and disruptive presence at each of the conferences. However, her age and her overheated rhetoric made her something of a caricature for most of those who attended, representing the worst of an oligarchy whose day had passed.

Gutiérrez and his colleagues spoke to our middle-class parishioners about the terrible discrepancies in Peru's social situation. They based their observations on Scripture, applying texts like "I was hungry and you did not give me anything to eat. . . ." (Matt. 25:42) to what was happening all around us. Each of the three evenings was structured to allow maximum participation from the audience, and the parish auditorium rocked with back and forth arguments about religion and politics, the role of the clergy in society, God's will for humanity (some of the well-to-do held the opinion that since there are hierarchies among the angels in heaven, there ought to be the same on earth). On and on the discussions raged. The priest presenters did not back down an inch from their own strongly held convictions, so that when the week concluded and the dust settled, we felt the debate had ended in something of a stalemate. I do not believe anyone's opinion of the place which faith has in society was changed. What was new, however, was the line in the sand that had been crossed.

I remember those three evenings in May of 1968 as the principal defining moment for the parish. It would never again be quite the same. It was true that from an unexamined, exclusive enclave of upper-middle-class parishioners, Most Holy Name was already, if gradually, becoming a place where questioning and analyzing the status quo in the light of the gospel and proclaiming Catholic social teaching were happening. As is always the case in such fundamental turnabouts, many experiences had already contributed to the approach of this conversion moment: the "red flags" of social inequities, mentioned in the previous chapter, for example; and the untenable policy of pastoral attention directed principally to the privileged class. Still, I am convinced that the conferences held at the parish in May of 1968 marked a definitive break with the old order of things and a turn to something completely new in Most Holy Name.

The fallout from this event was quite negative, at least in the short run. I calculated that about 80% of the middle-class parishioners disagreed intensely with Gutiérrez and his colleagues. It was clear that we had burnt some significant bridges by inviting these "radical" priests, and it remained to be seen what the lasting consequences of this would be.

Peruvian Priests' Group

As a result of this series of conferences at Most Holy Name by progressive members of the Peruvian clergy, they remembered to include me when they extended invitations to North American and European pastors to form part of their reflection groups. Later they told me that since I had not opposed giving them a hearing in a parish like Most Holy Name they had seen some possibilities in me. They felt I had taken a risk on their behalf. No other parish in any of Lima's middle-class residential areas extended a similar invitation. Of course it was the parish council that had come up with the idea to invite Gutiérrez and the others, but I got the credit. So a few months later I began to go to their meetings.

My participation in their weekly reflection sessions turned out to be an ongoing and invaluable education in the tools of social analysis and theological reflection. I had never before heard about, much less studied, these skills, and I took to them eagerly as just the kind of thinking I needed for the work at Most Holy Name. For the rest of my eleven years in Peru I remained a part of this priests' group. They helped me grow in my understanding of the social teaching of the church, especially the Latin American church, and in its consequences for pastoral efforts of every kind, especially parochial work.

This loosely organized priests' group called itself ONIS (in English: "The National Office for Social Investigation"), an acronym which quickly lost its original meaning as it never became an office, nor did the group engage much in investigative research. However, ONIS remained a recognizable designation for scores of progressive native and foreign priests in Peru who identified with the Medellín concepts and liberationist practices that were springing up across the Latin American church. As I shall mention later, I eventually had my difficulties with the ONIS group, but I stayed with it and found it to be a consistent source of inspiration and insight for my personal and prayer life as well as for our pastoral work in the parish. Their gatherings helped me to flesh out the Medellín vision.

Another member of ONIS was Peruvian-born Father German Schmitz of the Sacred Heart Congregation, and pastor of a parish very similar to Most Holy Name. Our common challenges in bringing the new thinking of the Peruvian Latin American church to upper-class parishioners brought us close together. German and I became good friends, and when he became auxiliary bishop of the Lima Archdiocese a year or so after the creation of ONIS, he was one of Most Holy Name's main supporters and defenders.

Bishop Schmitz was a shining example of the excellent bishops being named during that early post-Vatican II and Medellín period in the Latin American church. In addition to his duties in the archdiocese he chose to serve as pastor of a poor parish in the city, where he lived out the call for a preferential option for the poor. He traveled on public transportation, made himself accessible to everybody, especially to the poor, and supported at every turn the ever-deepening and radical social analyses taking place in all sectors of the faith communities in Lima. On one occasion when a wealthy person expressed concern that this new thrust of the Latin American church was helping the spread of communism, Bishop Schmitz responded that he was more worried about the actual presence of capitalism there and all the harm it was doing to people. Communism, he said, could be taken care of if and when it got its foot inside the door.

Each week we ONIS members who lived around the Lima area gathered to share our pastoral experiences with theologian Gustavo Gutiérrez, who served as the group's convener and principal commentator. These sessions were remarkable. For most of the two to three hours we spent together we talked about the day-to-day occurrences of pastoral life in our areas, the large and small stories of people in the parishes, the schools and our specialized pastoral groups. These experiences were really a chronicle of the struggles and tragedies, the successes and hopes, the joys and sorrows of the poor in that Third World city and country. At the conclusion of the sharing each week Father Gutiérrez would summarize what he had been hearing—not offering suggestions about pastoral approaches or solutions to problems expressed, but simply reflecting with us out of his own theological background. We began to hear Gutiérrez and the other priest-leaders around him talk about the need for a "political reading of the gospel." By this they meant going beyond the usual applications of God's Word to restricted individualistic situations, expanding them to include issues that affected the community and the wider society: political issues in the best sense of that term. The process Gutiérrez used, reflecting on our experiences and encouraging us to read the Scriptures in a "political way," was liberation theology in the making, although we did not as yet have a name for what we were doing.

The content and methodology of these weekly sessions always enriched those of us who participated in them. What increasingly struck me was this novel methodology Gutiérrez employed with the group week after week. He, the trained theologian, was the listener, giving us a little summary at the end of our sharing. I had never seen such a thing before. The theologians I knew, even those who were coming out of their studies with the new spirit of Second Vatican Council, were all in the habit of lecturing the rest of us. Life experience and questions always followed their erudite presentations. Here, however, was a trained theologian who actually wanted to hear what we had to say before giving us his thoughts. Gutiérrez would often tell us that our pastoral experiences provided him with the raw material for his thinking and writing.

One day, after many months of these weekly sessions, he made the observation that perhaps we (note the inclusion of everyone involved in the process) were crafting a new way of doing theology. He even ventured to name it—a theology of development. We took his observation at face value and without comment. Some weeks later, as I remember it, Gutiérrez returned to the subject of the "new" theology and said that it really wasn't a theology of development. That term, in his opinion, implied an already existing socioeconomic model, which the underdeveloped world would be expected to achieve. He said that our reflections on the lives of the people we served centered on the struggles of people, especially the poor, for a freer, more humane life, something he said was connected with the story of Exodus, where God called the people to move from slavery to freedom; he said that it was something having to do with liberation. I believe that was the first time this process of gospel reflection, which began with and centered on the experience of a people's striving for a better life, was called a theology of liberation.

For me this inductive from-the-bottom-up methodology—and its constant question of what our Judeo-Christian tradition has to say to "non-human beings"—made total sense. I had received a traditional, not to say an inadequate, theological education. I had been taught scripture, systematics and ethics not only as top-down applications of universal beliefs and rules for human conduct but principally as tools for refuting non-Catholic errors. Apologetics, explaining Catholicism to "outsiders," seemed to be the one overriding aim of the theological system I knew. The new thinking in the Catholic world, which came with Second Vatican Council and its *aggiornamento*, laid the foundation for the theological breakthrough I was experiencing with Father Gutiérrez. All was new—all was possible. But my encounter with this entirely new way of doing theology made all the possibilities come alive. It was a breath of fresh air for me.

Naturally my weekly participation in these conversations affected the conversion which was already taking place in Most Holy Name Parish. I would return from the gatherings of fellow pastors together with Father Gutiérrez and share the stories and reflections I had heard with the other Franciscans. Inevitably, the process, tone and content of the ONIS meetings extended to our parish council deliberations and ultimately became part of the mix for our policy decisions. The methodology of liberation theology proved enormously important for us. To my knowledge we never discussed any preaching theme, any parish policy, any new initiative without starting with the actual situation of our parishioners. For example, at one point a member of the parish council proposed that we put time and energy into improving the housing and general living situation of the caretakers on the construction sites in the parish. The initiative came out of our daily contact with these vulnerable people and from discussions about how the parish might help improve their subhuman living situations—liberation methodology. (We made serious efforts to have enforced the fairly progressive laws in Peru which regulated this situation, most of which ended in frustration. No one showed much interest in the plight of these poor, transient laborers. Looking back on this unsuccessful venture, I realize now that we needed a community organizer to show us how we could accomplish something for the caretakers.)

Opening to Other Influences

During these years we felt that almost wherever we looked there were forces pushing the avalanche of changes taking place at Most Holy Name. For example, one of the Peruvian priest leaders who had invited me into the ONIS group visited the parish one afternoon for lunch. In the course of our conversation he told me that many of the North American clergy serving in Peru were "just fooling around." He used the phrase in English for emphasis and went on to explain that these missionaries to his country were ignoring the underlying reasons for the oppressed situation of most Peruvians. Finally, he said, it would be better if they returned home rather than continue their superficial pastoral practices in Peru. In typically Latino style he did not include me explicitly in this devastating verdict. However, by this time I had come to understand enough of the mentality of South America to know that he really was speaking as much about me and the Franciscans at Most Holy Name as he was about "those North Americans." After my initial reaction of anger and defensiveness at this "insult" to me and my fellow North American missioners (I was, after all, still in the early stages of my own and the parish's conversion), I had to admit to myself the truth of what the man had said and share it with my brother Franciscans. Indeed, we had come to much the same conclusion about our own short history in Most Holy Name Parish and his comments about us pushed still further in the radicalization we all were experiencing.

Around the same time, the priests of several parishes, in what had come to be called the "residential deanery" (upper-middle-class sectors) of the archdiocese, elected me as their "dean"—a sort of area coordinator for pastoral sharing and planning. They evidently saw Most Holy Name as the most progressive and active parish in their sector and felt that I could provide some leadership for them. This position automatically placed me on the priests' senate of Lima, in touch with all dimensions of church life in the archdiocese. From that vantage point I saw clearly that not every parish was assimilating and putting the Medellín vision into practice.

Far from causing me second thoughts about what we were doing in Most Holy Name or influencing the other members of the parish council to call into question the parish's wholehearted embrace of Medellín at Most Holy Name, these examples of "business as usual," especially in the parishes of the privileged classes, strengthened our resolve to continue what had become a way of life with us. In fact, I felt rather sorry for the pastors and parishes who, for whatever reason—fear, lack of understanding, a reluctance to speak the prophetic word—avoided coming to grips with this mandate of the Latin American church. It struck me that parish life did not mean a great deal if it stuck to a spiritualized, otherworldly, unengaged model. Adopting and promoting the Medellín *línea* felt to us like absolutely the best thing we could do to make our parish relevant. It was also a clear call from the official church.

So we Franciscans and the parish council at Most Holy Name didn't spend much time worrying about the surrounding parishes. We had quite enough on our own plates as we implemented the new pastoral approaches of Medellín and its practical tools, liberation theology and conscientization. Later on, however, one particular event pointed up the growing differences between Most Holy Name and many of the other parishes in the affluent sector of Lima. Shortly after the brutal 1973 military coup of General Augusto Pinochet against the democratically elected Socialist government of President Salvador Allende in Chile, my friend Bishop Schmitz phoned me to inquire if our parish would be willing to receive refugees who were fleeing the repression in that country just to the south of Peru. Schmitz warned me that other parishes in our residential area had refused to take any refugees, for what he called their fear of "political consequences." Many of the Peruvian elites in parishes like Most Holy Name were finding common cause with the right wing government in Chile. My immediate response was: "Precisely because of the political consequences we will welcome these displaced people." I felt no need to consult my brother Franciscans or the parish council on the matter—our pastoral *línea* was clear, and I knew that they would applaud such a "political statement" on our part. In the ensuing months one or two refugee families and a well-known priest from Chile found sanctuary at Most Holy Name. The experience offered us Franciscans and others in the parish a privileged, if heartbreaking, place from which to view the tragedy taking place in their country.

The case of the Chilean priest who stayed with us illustrates the terribly repressive nature of the Pinochet regime. The man was a leading theologian in Chile, the leader of a group called "Christians for Socialism." When the military coup took place his name went on what was called the "A-List," of those to be shot on sight. The Archbishop of Santiago, Chile's capital city, negotiated a safe conduct for him to leave the country, and his friend Gustavo Gutiérrez asked us to house him at Most Holy Name.

During his two-month stay with us he was invited one Sunday to the home of a parishioner to have dinner with a visiting Chilean couple. The priest returned to the friary almost at once and explained that the husband of the couple was a colonel in the same Chilean Army which had issued the "shoot on sight" order against him and there was no way he could sit at table with the officer. To complicate the scene even further, it turned out that the Chilean couple was visiting as part of a delegation from the Christian Family Movement of their country—a prime example of the all-too-common disconnect between public and private morality.

Through all of these external and internal forces that were coming to bear on it, the parish moved dramatically from the generally innocent, unexamined place it had been in its first four years to a much more prophetic expression of church. What is interesting in retrospect is the fact that the day-to-day work of the parish did not change; its motivations and objectives did. Most Holy Name still carried out the traditional tasks of any modern Catholic parish but with a whole new emphasis and orientation. That shift and how it translated into parish practice lies at the heart of this entire story.

Preaching

The area of parish life that was immediately, deeply and lastingly affected most by the changes taking place was our preaching. Guided by all of the forces at play in the Latin American church—Medellín, liberation theology, Freire's conscientization method, ongoing social analysis and theological reflection—the Sunday homilies at Most Holy Name became a running commentary on local, national and international social realities in the light of Holy Scripture. In this important task of preaching the appropriate message Sunday after Sunday, the lay members of the parish council played a crucial role, assisting me and the other Franciscans with the right themes and examples. These well-informed men and women had also heard the message of Medellín on their own, or more often because of their involvement in the parish and the Lima Archdiocese, where so much change was happening. They came to a keen awareness of their privileged place in Peruvian society to the exclusion of most others there and to their great credit did not shrink from insisting that we address all of the scandalous situations which held this system in place.

One early example of this new line of preaching came when a parish council member read an article in *Time Magazine*, describing an elite wedding reception held in Biafra during the disastrous famine in that country. The writer described on the one hand the excess of gifts, food and imported alcoholic beverages lavished on the couple and their guests by the bride's wealthy father, and compared that scene with the starving children not two miles away from the wedding, their bellies swollen from malnutrition, bodies emaciated and covered with sores. In the following Sunday's homily, we read a translation of the *Time* article and made the point that one could substitute Peru for Biafra and Most Holy Name parishioners for the wedding guests, and be just as accurate.

Another homily commented on the long-expected news that with the discovery of large petroleum deposits in its northeastern jungle area, Peru had finally become an oil-producing country. A member of the parish council researched the economic situations of other oil-producing countries and found that they still showed terrible imbalances in per capita income and that most of them remained underdeveloped, except for the upper-class enclaves which were in some way connected into the petroleum wealth. In preaching about the discovery of oil in Peru, we wrapped these statistics around Biblical demands that wealth must be shared by all and that a nation is judged by how it treats the most vulnerable and needy of its citizens. This, we said, was a warning to our parishioners at Most Holy Name, many of whom would profit in one way or another from the recent oil find in their country.

It is important to note that in working on these weekly homilies we Franciscans and the parish council looked to the Holy Scriptures for our inspiration. We were not trying to be social pundits, interested only in commenting on the previous week's news. We tried to practice the kind of "political reading of God's Word" that liberation theology encouraged and that we practiced in the ONIS priests' group, opening the Hebrew and New Testament texts not only to individual circumstances but to the social realities surrounding all the members of the parish, as well as those of Peru and Latin America generally. In the examples cited above, the gospel which inspired the comparison between Biafra and Peru was the parable of the rich man and Lazarus; the biblical lesson about an oil rich society came right out of God's call for Jubilee Justice in Leviticus.

Initially, we Franciscans came on pretty strong in these homilies, in fact and in appearance. It was as if we and our "conscientized" parish council wished to make up for lost time—for the four previous years—during which we preached a consoling, essentially domesticating message. Also, it should be mentioned that we were foreigners, who were making serious and often negative observations about Peruvian and Latin American realities. In addition, of course we were speaking in Spanish, which meant not having at our command the nuanced or softened turn of phrase that would make the hard truths we were speaking a little more palatable. None of this was easy for the parishioners to accept, especially since they were accustomed to the friendly, unquestioning North Americans of the first years.

Gradually, however, we did make our homilies with their social commentaries much more integrated into what would be considered mainstream preaching. Once, after listening to a criticism from the cardinal that we were preaching too much on specific questions of social justice in our Sunday homilies, I went back and reviewed the records of a full year of homily themes. I found that while many of them did in fact address specific social issues, most themes followed appropriate topics for a given Sunday or liturgical season. The difference was that we now integrated the underlying and enveloping social dimension of any given theme or issue into our overall message.

Thus, for example, in a homily for a First Communion Sunday in the parish we preached about the beautiful image of children approaching the table of the Lord for the first time, expressing our thanks to the parents and teachers for preparing the little ones and asking for prayers that both parents and children would continue receiving the Bread of Life. But in that same homily we also might speak of the appropriate and essential dimension of the social consequences of Eucharist—that it is the sign of unity among God's still-divided people and a participation in the liberating act of Jesus by which all such division was radically challenged. For another example, in the Advent homilies we might highlight the centuries-long wait on the part of the Jewish people for the Messiah's first coming and also pointed to a similar attitude of waiting today for Christ's final coming. At the same time we could not overlook the words of the Our Father, "Thy Kingdom come," and pointed out the institutionalized violence standing in the way of Jesus' second coming.

As we went back over a year's homily themes in Most Holy Name it was clear that with the help of the parish council we had gotten past our initial tendency to concentrate on specific social ills as the theme for our homilies. We had integrated the church's social teaching, especially regarding Latin America, with the liturgical seasons and particular liturgical events throughout the year. This fact was duly reported to the cardinal. We felt we had calmed down a lot from those first weeks and months when this line of preaching began.

The Sunday homilies at Most Holy Name continued to be the way in which we expressed the pastoral turnaround that was taking place. We rarely preached a sermon which did not include some form of challenge to the social status quo around us and to our lifestyle as members of the privileged middle-class. This, of course, provoked responses and commentaries from the growing numbers of people attending Mass, as the parish grew numerically. We even had the case of a person who raised his hand during the homily and commented on what was being said. Afterwards I heard a parishioner say to another as they left the Mass that the pastor was crazy to let such an interruption happen. I felt, however, that all of these comments, even during the homily itself, were entirely appropriate. They rarely became nasty or polemical, thanks in large part to the natural graciousness of the Peruvian middle class, and they actually gave people a voice in matters about which good-willed people could disagree (as the saying goes). We continued to allow and even encourage these moments of dialogue.

Overall, the Sunday homily at Most Holy Name became the barometer for everything else that was taking place there.

The Parish School

As we continued the redirection of Most Holy Name Parish from a comfortable, upper-middle-class enclave to a prophetic and challenging expression of the Latin American church, the parochial school, now in its third year, came in for some scrutiny. Conducted by North American religious women (Sisters, Servants of the Immaculate Heart of Mary from Scranton, Pennsylvania) who were excellent educators, the school had quickly gained a well-deserved reputation for high academic standards, and the sisters ran it on a sound financial footing. Each year we constructed new classrooms as the school expanded. The waiting list of families hoping to get their children enrolled in the school testified to its reputation. As mentioned, however, the school catered exclusively to the children of those who could pay the substantial tuition costs required both to run it and continue construction of its physical plant. In effect, the school was a segregated educational center which discriminated against the children of poorer families in the parish solely on the basis of their economic status. On strictly human and Christian terms I never should have started the school in this way, as it was basically unjust from the beginning. Now, in light of the call issued at Medellín for a preferential option for the poor at every level of ministerial life and of all the other social forces impacting on the Peruvian church, there was a clear need for a change.

I felt that we had two choices, which I began to share with the sisters, the parish council and, gradually, the parents. Either the school should close its doors because it was a countersign to Jesus' message of inclusiveness for all God's children—or it should integrate into its classrooms the children of the poorer parishioners. I have to admit that I never seriously considered the first option. Rather, I pushed the idea that we would open the parish school to all the children of the parish. The sisters, the parish council and ultimately the middle-class parents, with varying degrees of enthusiasm, accepted my solution to our problem of segregation.

Naturally, the parents of children already attending Most Holy Name School presented the greatest challenge to the new policy we were implementing. A very enlightened president of the Parent Teachers Association—himself a member of the parish council—laid out the rationale and plan for integration at a special meeting of the Association. In order to bring the school into line with the gospel, with church teachings and with the pastoral priorities of Most Holy Name Parish (namely the preferential option for the poor), he told the parents that the school would thenceforth enroll the children of domestic workers and those of the caretakers on an equal footing with their own daughters and sons. Since the families of the poorer children in all likelihood could not afford school payments, he said, the well-to-do parents would have to pay at least double the present tuition in order for the school to continue on its solid economic footing.

Of course this was hard medicine for the parents to swallow. Both socially and financially, the integration of the classes in Peru went totally against the grain. With some notable exceptions, however, the members of the PTA, to their great credit, accepted this demanding arrangement, thanks no doubt to the excellence of the school itself and not incidentally to the Association president's compelling presentation. Within a year or two after the integration policy took effect, more than 30% of the school children came from the poor classes. And the school's economic health held firm.

One of the dissenters to the new school policy underscored the wrenching choice our decision to integrate the school posed for the parents. He highlighted the growing parish-wide reaction to the changes sweeping across Most Holy Name. The man was the parent of a girl in the third grade, one of the original and very satisfied members of the parish, really an excellent person whom I considered a close friend. He asked to speak with me one Sunday afternoon, shortly after the announcement of the integration policy. In our conversation he laid out most of the existing objections to what we were proposing for the school: a lowering of educational standards because of the presence in the classrooms of dull children whose parents could not supervise their studies, the danger of contagion from children who lived in such substandard housing with such terrible hygienic conditions, the bad language and perhaps bad morals which these unfortunate urchins could well bring with them from their deprived backgrounds.

After hearing out all of his objections, I asked my friend to put himself in my chair and look out across the street at the school, founded and conducted as an extension of parish ministry—indeed of Jesus' own ministry. What should be done, I asked him, if only those who could pay for them were allowed to share in the benefits of that educational opportunity carried on in the Lord's name? The response was dramatic and very painful, actually for both of us. The man literally lowered his head and agreed that integration was the only solution, then he walked out of my office. I knew that in spite of what he had said, his little girl would not continue in the parish school. To me it was a graphic modern example of the rich young man in Mark's gospel who had similarly gone away, sad in the face of Jesus' invitation to be a disciple because "he had many possessions" (Mark 10:22). I also knew that it was more than likely I would not see much of my friend again. That prediction proved true.

We were not unaware of the objections to integration, many of which were voiced by my friend that day. The children of the domestics and the caretakers did have serious handicaps. They were underdeveloped mentally, due to chronic hunger and the world of illiteracy they lived in. But thanks to the efforts of the sisters and lay teachers in the school, we began a nutritional and educational "head start" program for these little ones, feeding them breakfast before classes each day and working with them in vacation and summer school programs. We urged the domestics and the caretakers to do everything they could to send the children to school dressed in clean clothes, knowing that this would mean an extraordinary effort for these parents, many of whom had no regular access to clean water. We were not overly concerned about objections regarding bad language or improper behavior on the part of our newly integrated students. Our experience had shown that no particular economic level had a monopoly on bad words, and we knew that one of the strengths of our school was our supervision of all the children.

One quite unexpected bonus that flowed from the new policy came via the soccer field. With hardly any other form of recreational sport available to them, the poor children played soccer day and night. All they needed was some kind of a ball (often a bunch of rags tied together served this purpose) and a bit of open space. They all played extremely well and became the stars of a burgeoning sports program at the school. Of course this made the poor kids popular with their "peers" from the wealthy sectors.

On balance, the integration of Most Holy Name School proved enormously successful. The overwhelming majority of well-to-do parents accepted it and in time embraced it as a healthy experience for their children. The children themselves hardly noticed any change in their classroom complexion. And of course the parents of the poor children were ecstatic that their little ones had a chance at real schooling.

Lifestyle

A very important and sensitive area of impact on the parish as the Medellín vision took hold had to do with lifestyle questions. The living standards of the privileged class at Most Holy Name Parish, beginning with us Franciscans, had to be seriously reviewed in the face of the church's call for a "preferential option for the poor." Out of a sense of basic integrity, I felt that we needed to reassess our own lives and luxuries, such as having our own cars or going out to dinner at upscale restaurants or accepting invitations to exclusive clubs, all in the framework of the Third World setting in which we were living. How could we go on Sunday after Sunday preaching about the social discrepancies in the parish and continue our own upper-middle-class lifestyle? So, gradually we changed habits which we had theretofore taken for granted and took on more appropriate lifestyle expressions for pastoral workers in an essentially impoverished world.

For example, I came to the conclusion with some embarrassment (which continues till today) that my North American clerical custom of the sacrosanct free day, complete with a round of golf, dinner at an upscale restaurant and perhaps a movie in the company of other U.S. priests, was a glaring contradiction. How could I go around six days each week speaking about and acting on the Medellín vision of equality for all and on the seventh engage in activities which reeked of privilege? It wasn't long before the entire group of my priest friends came to the same conclusion and we dropped the golf and restaurants in favor of less ostentatious pastimes.

In the context of that post-Medellín moment, that decision about free days and the golf/dinner/movie routine proved fairly painless. It sort of fell on us by the weight of its own logic. In the end it taught me a life-long lesson. A short time after putting an end to the weekly golf games, I found myself going on an errand which took me past the swanky country club where I used to play. As I drove by, I glanced out the window of the car (which I still had) and looked over the well-manicured, grassy fairways of the golf course where I had spent many hours. In that instant I noticed on the dusty shoulder of the roadway, outside of the fence which barred entry to the club, a poor, Indigenous family having a little picnic of coca-cola and potato chips. The tableau was not lost on me: I still had my own car and my own privileged place as an educated, North American priest; now at least I knew that I had chosen to situate myself on the outside of the fence, where the poor find themselves. And that was the right side of the fence for me. It was clear to me that this would have to be my life's goal from then on: to try as best I could to stand with those who never could hope to enjoy access to the real and metaphorical golf courses of this world.

Some of our lifestyle decisions came hard. Around this time my fellow Franciscans at Most Holy Name decided among themselves that we needed a new car. Without my knowing it, they went ahead, researched the various makes and models which we might buy and decided on one in particular. At one of our weekly community meetings these brothers presented me with the results of their investigations as pretty much a done deal. My immediate reaction was to stall for time—time for all of us to judge both the need for a car and the effect which buying a new one would have on our overall pastoral approach at Most Holy Name. The brothers granted me the week of reassessment which I asked for, and when the next community meeting rolled around they told me that they had come to the conclusion that the new car idea just wasn't feasible.

These personal and communal reflections about our own lifestyle inevitably called into question the way our middle- and upper-middle-class parishioners lived. From the beginning of the parish one of the great sources of unity and indeed pride in the parish, at least among the privileged, was our enthusiastic participation in their active social life. Perhaps this sense of satisfaction with our engagement in the parties and fiestas arose to some extent at least because the presence of a priest or religious legitimated in some way the excesses of an elite wedding reception, or a birthday or anniversary celebration; perhaps it was because the people simply enjoyed having their young North American priests and sisters at these functions. In any case, our questioning of such lifestyle habits, which became increasingly pointed, resulted in a kind of break in the parish unity which these social events had helped create.

The changes made by us Franciscans caused the parishioners a certain unease about their own lifestyles. My discontinuation of the weekly golf game, for example, brought up questions like: does this mean that golf is bad? Are you suggesting that all of us should drop activities like golf? And why are you denying yourself legitimate recreation? It is my recollection that critiques of our comfortable parishioners' living standards were done more often by our example rather than directly. They found their mark in any case as they contrasted the privileged place we had in Peruvian life with the grinding poverty endured by the other social classes represented in the parish. From time to time, of course, we spoke quite directly to this glaring imbalance.

One new arrival in the parish called to ask me if I would bless his recently completed home. These house blessings among the privileged classes typically kicked off extravagant parties, complete with live orchestras, uniformed waiters, guests in formal or semiformal attire, with food and drinks in abundance. They were opportunities for the owner of the new home to display one-upmanship in that competitive social pecking order that was upper-middle-class Lima. The house to be blessed on this occasion belonged to the army general in charge of what was an enormously lucrative fishing industry at that time in Peru. Given his government portfolio, the general's fiesta would by social demand have to be several notches above most of those offered by his peers.

On the evening of the blessing and fiesta I walked the short distance from the parish house to the general's residence, taking note along the way of the several construction sites where the impoverished caretakers and their families lived their miserable existence. I was met at the door by the general in the customary, very gracious Latino fashion and invited to proceed inside for the ritual. I stayed in the doorway, however, and described what I had just seen of other Peruvians eking out pitiable lives, alongside grand houses like the general's. I told the host that I would gladly bless his home right there in the entranceway but that because of the poverty right outside of where we were, I really could not take part in the rest of the festivities, which were already gathering momentum. Again, in that typically cordial Latin style the general smoothly called the guests to the door, explaining that the *padre* would not be participating in anything more than the blessing, and all stood quite respectfully while the prayers were said and the holy water sprinkled. I never saw the new parishioner again.

I sat at a traffic light near the parish one day and noticed one of our parishioners in the car next to me. The woman appeared to be alone in her late model vehicle but when I looked again I saw her domestic worker, sitting silently in the back seat. No interaction was taking place between the lady and her servant. The significance of the scene was not lost on me—separated social classes and the obvious power imbalance even between two women who lived under the same roof. That snapshot of a particular household gave me a starting point for a forthcoming Sunday homily on relationships in the parish "community."

During those years in Peru a reformist government put severe restrictions on all private possession of foreign currencies. Everyone in the country had to turn in American dollars or deutsche marks or British pounds sterling and receive the equivalent in Peruvian money. The government's objective was to collect valuable exchanges like the dollar into the national treasury so that it could service the growing debt owed by Peru to international lending agencies. Many well-to-do Peruvians, instead of handing in their foreign money, used any number of ingenious means to sneak their money out of the country to overseas bank accounts. One story circulated about a Peruvian businessman who attempted to leave Peru for a trip to New York, only to be stopped by the police at Lima's airport. They had received a tip that the cast he had on an allegedly fractured arm was only there to conceal a large stash of dollars. Over the man's protests the police insisted on cutting away the cast—and found nothing. In all this confusion the businessman missed his flight and of course made a scene about lost time and missed appointments. The police apologized profusely and twenty-four hours later practically escorted him onto the next flight to New York, which he boarded with a great show of offended dignity. This time the repaired cast held thousands of U.S. dollars.

As I was leaving for a visit to the United States around this time, a very close friend asked me to take a large quantity of dollars with me and deposit it in a bank account he had in the States. For me this was just as much a lifestyle question as any other. I refused my friend's request because I felt that these restrictions on foreign currencies were a justified form of income tax. To squirrel away wealth in another country ultimately hurt Peru, especially the poorest there.

Around that time Lima's cardinal, motivated by what he and the other bishops had called for at the Medellín Conference, announced that he would move from his impressive residence on one of the most prestigious avenues in Lima to a more modest home in a lower-middle-class neighborhood. This gesture on the cardinal's part evoked the same questions that were being voiced in Most Holy Name: what are you asking us to do by this lifestyle change? Is everyone expected to lower their living standards? The cardinal handled it with remarkable calm and conviction. In effect he said: I am doing what I feel is right—you will have to decide for yourselves what you are called to do. His response echoed pretty much what we were saying at Most Holy Name: each of us has to decide for ourselves what we can and must do to eliminate the scandalous gap in living conditions across our society.

Looking back, I believe that it was probably these lifestyle challenges which most disturbed and divided the members of Most Holy Name. They seemed to hit at the heart of upper-middle-class identity. In fact, it was true that many of these well-to-do folks had worked hard to achieve their privileged status; none was what would be called "filthy rich," or playboy types who had inherited fortunes from their parents and grandparents. Some of the middle-class folks had even come out of near-poverty and could call themselves self-made. Even these people, however, had rarely experienced the crushing and paralyzing poverty of the masses in Peru. The Medellín call for an option on behalf of the poor, together with the lifestyle changes involved in that option, touched very sensitive nerves with our middle-class parishioners. They didn't like to hear that message and reached for all sorts of rationalizations to excuse themselves from its implications.

One of the most frank discussions I remember having on the subject of lifestyle revolved around the question of "What good will the poor get out of any change I make in my standard of living?" Given the enormity of the poverty suffered by vast numbers of people all over Latin America, this argument had a lot of merit. Very few people would say that if each wealthy person sacrificed a large portion of his or her assets on behalf of the poor, injustice would be overcome. The problem of generalized poverty in Peru and all over the Third World was so much more complicated and related to all kinds of national and international structures. Still, the Medellín documents had spoken to this very point, and in this and so many discussions like it I resorted to their argument. Speaking about voluntary poverty in the church itself and in the lives of church people, the bishops said: "Poverty [is] a commitment through which one assumes voluntarily and lovingly the conditions of the needy of this world in order to bear witness to the evil which they represent and to spiritual liberty in the face of material goods. . . ." (Medellín, "Poverty of the Church"). The architects of Medellín left very little wiggle room in calling the whole church to solidarity with the poor, and we at Most Holy Name felt obliged as well as empowered to preach this line particularly through our own example.

The Sacramental Life of the Parish

Curiously, I have little memory of the way we applied the Medellín vision to our sacramental ministry, as that vision came into focus at Most Holy Name. This is strange because obviously we came to understand that a correct celebration of the Eucharist calls into question the inequitable sharing of bread among God's children: that was precisely the scandal in this parish of plenty and scarcity. The rite of reconciliation, we knew, is supposed to challenge situations, like ours at Most Holy Name, of unreconciled social realities—the home owners in relation to their domestic help or the near-palatial homes built next to straw huts. We could see that welcoming new life into the community of faith through baptism had to raise questions about the quality of life for all members of that community—a quality that was enormously uneven in the parish. Indeed, each sacrament carries a social price tag.

The famous case of a Colombian priest at that time served to illustrate this important point. Father Camilo Torres of the Archdiocese of Bogotá left the priesthood in 1965, convinced that he could not "offer the gifts at the altar" (Matt. 5:23) until he had done something effective to bridge the gap between the privileged and underprivileged classes in his country. He joined one of Colombia's guerrilla movements and was killed shortly thereafter in a military skirmish. As we reflected on Torres's experience, it was clear that his extreme way of "leaving his gift at the altar and going to be reconciled with his offended sister or brother," while heroic and even prophetic, was not something we could imitate. If it were imitated, who could ever celebrate the Eucharist or the other sacraments? We all know people who have something against us. And in terms of "institutionalized sin" we know that we owe huge debts to whole classes of people. We bring our gifts to the altar as sinners in a broken world. However, Father Torres did make a powerful (prophetic) statement about the social "price tag" on the church's sacramental life.

Yet there is no memory of such explicit reflections in our distribution of the sacraments at Most Holy Name during that period of change or thereafter. One possible reason for this might lie in the fact that we actually made these connections only implicitly. Certainly, as mentioned, the preaching in the parish consistently highlighted the great themes celebrated by each of the sacraments—bread for the journey of liberation, reconciliation based on justice, initiation into a "conscientized" Christian community, marital love as a gift, and commitment to a hurting world. The social implications of every sacrament were folded into our presentation and celebration of them. Perhaps we Franciscans and the parish council considered this sufficient. We did hear of a particular Peruvian priest, very radical and almost extremist in his views for sure, who refused to baptize one of his nieces because of the family's position of privilege. It was an action which none of us at Most Holy Name ever considered. I continue to wonder what more we and the parish council could have done in our sacramental ministry.

Ever Pastoral

As all of these changes of approach took place at Most Holy Name, the original ideal of pastoral care for all people who came to the parish remained firmly in place. We Franciscans and the sisters who staffed the school continued to visit the homes of parishioners, tend to the sick, offer a growing variety of sacramental and other spiritual services and carry out the various renewals called for by the Second Vatican Council.

As an example of our expanding ministries, a group of upper-middle-class parishioners with severely mentally and physically disabled children approached me to inquire about first Eucharist for their little ones. The task of bringing these special girls and boys to a minimum awareness of this sacrament proved formidable. You would wonder at times if a particularly handicapped child had any grasp of what the Eucharist meant. Still, in our eyes and certainly in the eyes of their loving parents, they were God's special favorites. So the celebration of their First Holy Communion proved a wonderfully affirming and healing event in their lives, and a great consolation for their parents. For several years we worked with successive groups of these families and celebrated the sacrament with them and their precious little ones.

On one occasion, a successful physician who lived in the parish suffered a fatal heart attack in his home. (Actually, the man had been doing his rounds at the hospital where he worked and, incredibly, drove himself home when he began to experience chest pains.) In all the confusion of the moment, the doctor's wife instinctively called me to anoint her husband before calling for a doctor. Almost exactly the same scenario played out later on in the case of an architect who died at home in the middle of the night. His wife, too, came for our help first. We understood such actions, taken at moments of extreme need, as acknowledgments that the priests and religious of the parish, for all our unpopular social analyses and critiques, stood ready at all times to serve every member of the community.

Some years into the post-Medellín era at Most Holy Name, the parish council decided to conduct a poll among the parishioners regarding their opinion about the parish. Each council member took the time to visit several homes and asked the people a series of questions regarding the parish and its ministers, and especially the parishioners' degree of satisfaction with the overall service offered at Most Holy Name. While many responded with varying levels of dissatisfaction with respect to the emphasis on social issues in our approach to ministry, there was almost unanimously positive feedback about the good will and attentive service offered by us Franciscans and the sisters. People appreciated the fact that for all our "political" concerns, we never stopped being their pastors.

Of course, from my point of view and that of all who were ministering at Most Holy Name, including the parish council, especially, the whole move away from the pacifying and consoling approach of the first years was itself an effort to be more pastoral and more concerned about the life of every parish member, rich and poor. The preaching of the full gospel, applying God's word not only on the life of each individual but also on the sum of those realities which affect every aspect of his or her life, is, after all, the central point of this story. We came to understand such full gospel application as a pastoral demand. Once this was understood, we realized there was no way we could ever again return to anything less. I will make this point in greater detail in chapter 11.

CHAPTER 6

Option for the Poor
in Most Holy Name

At the same time that the original pastoral thrust of Most Holy Name Parish—with attention given principally to the upper classes—was undergoing this radical reorientation, we had to face real questions about the poorer sectors which we had mostly neglected in the parish—the domestic workers and the caretakers. We knew that the Medellín vision of a preferential option for the poor and a change of those structures which had created and held in place the impoverished majorities in Latin America required more than the pastoral tokenism which had marked our service to them. The assessment mentioned in a previous chapter of North American pastoral ministers "just fooling around" and not addressing the underlying causes of underdevelopment and marginalization stuck in my mind. I had to admit that in the first years at Most Holy Name we had practiced a preferential option for the privileged. We had to remedy this situation and offer the right kind of pastoral attention to the poor among our parish members.

The Domestic Workers

During the watershed year of 1968 we took a first significant step toward this goal. The integration of the parish school spurred me to think about the educational needs of the domestic workers, most of whom had little or no formal education and no practical way to acquire schooling. Since the day students finished their school day early in the afternoon and left the classrooms empty for the rest of the day, there was no reason why a second parochial school could not function in the later afternoon and evening hours, to serve these young workers. Under the capable direction of one of my Franciscan colleagues and with a completely different corps of teachers from the morning school, we began the *vespertina* (night school).

This venture turned out to be an immediate success. The domestic workers saw the night school as the opportunity of a lifetime—formal primary and secondary education close to their places of employment, conducted by their parish at minimum cost. The workers did pay a nominal tuition, but the bulk of the expenses for the night school were, almost incredibly, covered by earnings from the already-burdened, integrated day school. The financial success of the *vespertina* put me in mind of Jesus' feeding five thousand; we seemed able to feed a great number of students in both our schools with the proverbial five loaves and two fish. The fact that these young women and men flocked to the *vespertina* spoke volumes about their instinctive understanding of the value that education could have in their lives. The school flourished from the beginning.

In contrast to our previous custom of holding monthly social gatherings, we now had daily and much more relevant contact with the domestic workers in the night school. This new relationship quickly uncovered another area of pastoral concern—a sort of fatalistic attitude among them about their lives as domestic workers. Most of these young women and men, despite grudging permission on the part of their employers to attend the evening classes, continued to live and work under near slave-like conditions. While they were generally aware of their oppressed lives, we felt a need to stir up in these fairly passive workers a true conscientization in the dynamic of Paulo Freire, one that would push them toward actions against the institutionalized sin they suffered.

Since none of us priests and religious at Most Holy Name had serious training in an appropriate pedagogy which would help marginalized people like our domestic workers, the Franciscan brother who served as principal of the night school turned for help to an archdiocesan organization that had training and experience with such methods, the Young Christian Workers. In this we lucked out. With their well-known "see, judge and act" approach to situations of injustice and discrimination, the YCW worked in teams, consisting of a woman religious, a priest and—very importantly—one or two very aware and alert domestic workers who could relate perfectly to their peers in situations like those of the workers in the residences around Most Holy Name Parish. It turned out to be a perfect match.

We had the ideal infrastructure—a large parish house and a safe environment—as well as an obvious willingness to offer any help we could to the YCW trainers in their crucial work. For their part, the Young Christian Workers saw the opportunity offered by Most Holy Name as a perfect proving ground for their ongoing efforts to raise both the consciousness and ultimately the living standards of their oppressed sisters and brothers. The process proved fascinating and ultimately most successful.

Very late each Saturday night, when the domestics had finally finished another long day of cleaning and cooking, large numbers of them—as many as twenty or thirty—would come by invitation to the parish house and spend the entire night there. Of course this meant that the young domestic workers lost a whole night's sleep, a real sacrifice for them given the long hours and tediousness of their working lives. With help from the YCW team, the domestics would carry on a variety of activities. In the beginning, for example, one of these was a weekly game of some sort—volleyball, basketball, parlor games—played indoors or out according to weather conditions, by all who showed up. After the game the entire group would gather to reflect on the game, discussing the various roles played by each of them—who organized the teams, who provided the balls and nets that were used, who played an active and who played a passive role in the game as participant or spectator, who encouraged the others during the game, who helped with the cleanup, etc.

The objective of this weekly reflection on the games played was to establish individual identity—to show the workers that each of them had a distinct personality with his or her own gifts and with different talents for participating in these group activities. This first step in the conscientization process was crucial for these young people who had never thought of themselves or been treated as individuals, especially in the homes of the wealthy. They were simply "la chica—el chico" (the girl—the boy), persons without identity, clothed in drab aprons, allowed to be in the house only to carry out the menial chores which the rest of the family considered below them. Over the weeks and months the YCW worked with the domestics we saw the simple process of playing games and above all reflecting on the dynamics of the games gradually bringing these young women and men to a knowledge of themselves as distinct persons with individual gifts. It was fascinating to observe.

Gradually, as the Saturday night to Sunday morning gatherings continued over the following months and years, the YCW trainers directed the process to the domestics' awareness of their living and working conditions in each of their households, the treatment dealt them by the homeowners and the powerlessness they felt in a market saturated with young people just like them. They reflected how the lady of the house thought of them as if they were expendable or interchangeable parts, thanks to so many others like them who also needed jobs. Placed alongside the workers' growing sense of their own personhood and dignity, these insights proved truly "conscientizing"—helping them see the structural injustices which surrounded their lives.

As noted in explaining the Freire methodology in chapter 6, the YCW trainers did not give lectures to the domestic workers about their own individual dignity, nor about their essentially unjust working conditions. This would have violated the principle underlying the entire notion and genius of conscientization as something one does for oneself. The trainers simply asked the right questions and the domestics took it from there.

The conscientization sessions also dealt with the workers' view of dignified and dignifying labor. In a society which undervalued physical work, especially among the middle and upper classes, the domestics began to understand that all labor can be a positive force in their lives—it depends on how the worker understands it. They came to take pride and satisfaction in carrying out their assigned tasks around the house as well as possible. The result was that those who continued with the YCW method gradually became recognized by the home owners as the best domestic employees in the neighborhood.

Because of their servants' improved work ethic the upper-middle-class folks did not seem to mind, much less oppose, what their domestic employees were experiencing each week at the parish house. The fact that the workers gradually came to see their tasks not as drudgery but as honest and dignifying labor and become better at their jobs helped the homeowners resign themselves to yet another Medellín-inspired innovation in their parish. The former resistance to domestics' gathering at the parish house and comparing notes about their working situations just melted away.

A major breakthrough took place at this juncture. With the awareness that they were now respected as good workers and even sought after by the homeowners, these conscientized young domestics decided to form a union. Despite all the work being done by the Young Christian Worker teams, too many of the workers' peers still faced oppressive conditions in the middle-class homes. A union, they thought, would offer protections for all of them. However, Peruvian law did not contemplate the possibility of a union comprised of domestic workers, since these workers had multiple and independent employers. So these now quite confident domestics managed to have the law modified to fit their special circumstances. With their union they now could hold all their employers accountable for the treatment of each domestic worker. If one of them was mistreated, the threat of all domestic workers going out on strike provided what might be called "corrective leverage" among all the homeowners. The ladies did not want to lose their good workers because of mistreatment by others of their class.

This transformation of dozens of domestic workers from timid, almost invisible drones working in the homes of the middle class to the alert, self-confident young labor agitators in a few short years was really astounding for us at Most Holy Name. We would not have dreamed it possible had we not seen it for ourselves. We were impressed, too, with the gospel dimension of the whole process, the consistent references in the YCW method to God's Word and God's call for universal liberation. From the first tentative steps in getting the workers to see themselves as individual persons, all the way to their plans and programs for initiatives like a labor union and outreach to their peers within and outside Most Holy Name, the YCW teams continually brought in the spiritual or liberating dimensions of what was happening. On one or two occasions I witnessed the inspiring celebrations of the Eucharist early on Sunday mornings as these young people prepared to return to their work places. They seemed to understand clearly that in celebrating Jesus' own death and rising, his triumph over injustice, they were celebrating the movement from death to life happening then and there in their own lives and environment.

The Caretakers

Many children of the most neglected class of people in the parish, the caretakers living on the ever-increasing number of construction sites, had received scholarships when the integration of the parochial school took place. This delighted the caretakers, who saw education as an escape route from poverty for the children and through their children ultimately for themselves.

We made some efforts at conscientization among the caretakers. This was hard work because these struggling people did not have much time or energy for the discussion sessions, which were usually held in the evenings. However, we did use the fact that their children now went to the parochial school and the parents' interest in education for their daughters and sons as a way to reach them. At best, however, these sessions were sporadic and never really satisfied the enormous need for consciousness-raising among the caretakers. Still, the dialogues we were able to have often revealed the potential that was there among these totally marginalized folk.

One evening at a gathering of several poor parents, I proposed a case for discussion. I told them about the actual experience of a young Peruvian factory employee who began some active union organizing among his fellow workers. When the factory owners noticed these activities, they tricked him into leaving the factory floor by offering the young man a job in management. Now, they told him, he would go to work each day dressed in a collar and tie (the uniform of the middle class); instead of a lunch pail he would eat in the dining room reserved for the overseers; and he would have his own office. However, he was given little or nothing to do. When the young man realized what was happening and how management had co-opted him with the perks of a higher but meaningless job, he resigned his position and went back to the factory floor.

When I finished telling the story, I posed the conscientizing question: what did the poor parents think of the young worker's decision? To a person they answered that the man was out of his mind to leave the comfortable position he had been given. He should have stayed in his little office and enjoyed life. It was not the answer which I was hoping for, but seemed to be the consensus among those gathered. In the conscientization method, the leader cannot violate the process by imposing the "correct" interpretation, so I felt I might have to content myself with their conclusion that evening.

However, as so often happened in these sorts of conversations, one of the participants timidly raised his hand and quietly declared that he thought the young organizer was a hero—"a hero to our class" were his words. The rest of the assembly got it immediately and the whole conversation turned to a discussion of the positive consequences of such an outstanding act for the oppressed classes of Peru. It was "conscientization" at its most effective—and, I felt, its most "dangerous." The impoverished parents sitting in that group came to realize that the education of their children in the parish school could not be solely for their family's individual betterment. In that short discussion they had gained a sense that class loyalty was the goal—that the example of the heroic young worker meant that none of them would be truly liberated until all of them were. For these poor folks it was a dramatic and truly sobering insight. I came away from the session deeply moved by the power and the really demanding consequences which conscientization held for this oppressed class of people. Given the conclusions they had come to, I wondered if leaving them ignorant of those consequences wasn't better. And yet, even as I thought it, I knew ignorance could never be the right way.

Knowing the Poor

Despite the occasional opportunities to sit down and reflect with them, I never felt satisfied that the caretakers received adequate ministerial attention in the sense of a "conscientization" which would lead to the kind of structural changes which the domestic workers were making. As the parish continued its efforts toward a preferential option for the poor, the steps we took to serve the watchmen and their families remained principally on the level of charity—assistance programs to help them deal with the daily challenges of basic survival. Despite the fact that these initiatives seldom reached the level of social analysis or social change for the caretakers, they did a great deal of good and helped all of us on the pastoral team at Most Holy Name to experience at close range the lives of the poorest members of the parish, indeed those of Peruvian society in general.

The Medical Post

One of the charitable ministries we undertook to serve these very poor parishioners was the establishment of a medical post in the large basement of the parish auditorium. This was an early initiative I started with the help of two generous doctors who agreed to take turns working afternoon hours at the post several days each week. When we turned our more focused attention toward the poorer sectors of the parish the medical post became one of our major outreach efforts, especially toward the caretakers and their families. A sister from the Immaculate Heart of Mary community arrived in Peru to join the faculty of the parish school. When I learned that she was also a registered nurse, I insisted over the objections of the other teachers that she take over the medical post full time. I felt we could not forego this sister's expertise as a medical professional particularly at the time when we were devoting more and more of our attention to the needs of the poorest parishioners. Thanks to her interest in the poor and skill as a nurse, we expanded our attention to this indigent population with its seemingly endless variety of illnesses. With a religious woman running it, the medical post became an efficient and welcoming place where the poor came for first aid. It also served as an early detection center for serious cases, which we would then refer to the more sophisticated health facilities in the city.

From the beginning, Most Holy Name Parish had enjoyed a reputation for kindness toward the poorer sectors of its population, even

though in hindsight our early efforts seemed to us like tokenism. Now
with the integration of poor children in the parochial school, the
vespertina and the upgraded medical post there was institutional evidence of that ministerial concern, especially in the eyes of the poor
themselves. They began to come to the parish in large numbers with
all sorts of requests, and we did what we could to help them. However, we knew that daily contact with these oppressed, needy,
marginalized Peruvians benefited us Franciscans and the sisters at
least as much. The whole Latin American church, especially the insights of liberation theology taught us the privileged place these "little
ones" have in God's eyes and in the broad sweep of salvation history.
We came to know "the least of the brothers and sisters," often by
their names, along with their hopes and despairs, their tragedies and
their rare small victories, and we understood a little better why Jesus
is quoted in Matthew's gospel as identifying with them ("As often as
you have done this to the least of my brothers and sisters, you have
done it to me" [Matt. 25:405]).

One Christmas Eve, just as I was preparing to celebrate Midnight
Mass, a knock came at the door of the parish house. A poor boy of
nine or ten years stood crying in the doorway, pleading with me and
pulling my arm, to come and attend his sick mother. I walked with
the lad the short distance to their "house," a typical shack on a construction site, expecting the worst. Too often the poor would send for
help when it was too late. But when I entered the place, I saw at once
that the mother was not sick at all but had just given birth to a healthy
baby with her husband attending her. The little boy had panicked at
hearing his mother's cries during labor and had run to get help from
the *padre*. I had my Christmas homily, not only because of the immediate happy ending of the little drama, but also because of its lesson
for the privileged Mass-goers: the Christmas story continues with
another (Peruvian) child born into the poverty which Jesus encountered at his birth and which he calls us to overcome. When I returned later on Christmas day to check on the newborn and her
mother, there was no sign of the little family. They had simply cleared
out. I never saw them again. Later, when I reflected on the incident,
I remembered how bright it had been inside the shack. They had
lighted a very efficient Coleman gas lamp for the birthing process—

still I was struck at how illuminated the little room had been.

As our sister-nurse walked the few blocks to her home late one afternoon after a day at the medical post, she sensed someone walking behind her trying to get her attention. She looked around and saw a poor woman silently holding out a newly born and desperately sick child in the throes of convulsions. The sister rushed mother and child to the emergency room of a local hospital and insisted on immediate treatment of the days-old baby for tetanus. Thanks to that quick action and an extended hospital stay the baby survived.

Later we reflected on the passive attitude of the mother. Instead of screaming at the nurse to do something about her child's condition, she walked behind her, hoping that the sister would notice her. Oppressed and marginalized people, we found, so often act that way. They have accepted the "fact" that they count for very little in this world.

The sister and I decided to investigate what might have caused such a life-threatening infection in the newborn. The mother told us that when her labor pains began, she went by public transportation to the city's maternity hospital only to be told that, since she had not undergone pre-natal care, they would not admit her. Still in labor, the woman took the bus back to the hut where she and her family lived and delivered the baby with her husband helping out. When it came time to cut the umbilical cord, he did it with a sharp stone that was lying on the dirt floor. End of mystery about the tetanus infection and the beginning of yet another reflection in the parish about structural injustices like subhuman housing, lack of basic education in pre- and postnatal care, and the need for a more compassionate medical establishment.

One day I took two babies in a serious state of dehydration to a local clinic run by a congregation of Catholic sisters and, confident that the children would receive the necessary attention, left them in the emergency room with their mother. A day later I went by the house where the children lived to see how they had made out and found both babies back in bed there, still quite seriously ill. The mother explained that the sisters had told her there was no room in the clinic and she had been sent home. I took the children to a city hospital, where they finally received treatment, and then decided to test the "no vacant bed" story of the sisters. I asked one of the middle-class parishioners to phone the clinic and in her most upper-class Spanish ask that her own "dehydrated" child be admitted to the clinic. The sister responded by asking if the lady wanted a private or semiprivate room. The ensuing confrontation between me and the religious was not pretty, as I promised police intervention should such discrimination ever happen again.

These encounters with the poorest of the poor women and men who now flocked to Most Holy Name put flesh and blood on the documents of Medellín. Our option for the poor became personalized, no longer a question of a generic group called "the poor," but of the Olgas, the Antonias and the Tomases (all real persons) whom we came to know by name and by the circumstances of their lives. Increasingly, the preaching and actions of the parish were done from the side of, from the experience of, in the name of each poor person we priests and religious encountered on a daily basis. Indeed, being the voice of the voiceless became the hallmark of every aspect of Most Holy Name—our preaching, our lifestyle, our budget, the administration of the schools, right down to the equal treatment of poor and privileged alike in questions of sacraments and other pastoral attention. Occasionally I would find myself amused by the reaction of a well-to-do parishioner as he or she entered the parish office expecting immediate attention, only to be told that I would see him or her after some domestic worker or caretaker.

Still, as noted, the pastoral work we carried out with these "little ones," the caretakers, never seemed enough: perhaps it never could have been enough, given the sheer numbers of impoverished individuals in the parish and its environs. Naturally, the poor people did not know anything about parish boundaries; they came to Most Holy Name because the parish had a growing reputation for kindness—institutionalized kindness, if you will—toward them. Nevertheless, I would always feel that the Medellín call for the kind of "preferential option for the poor" that would lead to structural change by and for the poor themselves fell short at Most Holy Name. In this I may have allowed the overwhelming and intractable poverty of a Third World city and country to depress me. How indeed could the efforts of one parish, even with all the good will in the world, make a significant dent in the "institutionalized sin" of that world?

This dilemma, if it can be called that, came home dramatically to us Franciscans and the sisters one evening as we came together for one of our occasional "team meetings." As we began to share our thoughts about the various ministries in which we were engaged, the sister-nurse who ran the medical post spoke of the endless line of sick poor she attended each day. She reasoned that even were she able to help cure every one of those patients, that line would never get shorter. Poverty and its byproduct, chronic sickness, are a deadly combination in underdeveloped countries like Peru. (The word "underdeveloped" is not politically correct today. People prefer "developing countries" or "nations on the way to development." These, however, are euphemisms, falsehoods really, because most of the global south today remains as poor if not poorer than ten, twenty or forty years ago. On the other hand, as we learned when Father Gutiérrez was searching for the right word to describe his and our "bottom-up" process of theologizing, development—and underdevelopment—are problem words as well. They imply some predetermined model to which countries need to aspire in seeking a dignified life for their people.) The sister then asked the rest of us on the team: "In the lives of those unfortunate women, men and children, where is the evidence of a loving God who, Jesus told us, cares for His/Her children more than the lilies of the field and the birds of the air?" As she expressed what had become for her a real crisis of faith, all of us in the group had to ask ourselves the same question, since each of us knew exactly what the sister was experiencing. It was a long while—weeks? months?—before we discerned that each of us, and all who follow Jesus, have to be the evidence of that loving and caring God—or else no such evidence exists. In a nutshell, this reflection summed up the message of the Latin American church at the Medellín Conference.

So while I was never satisfied that we were doing all that could be done, I did know that our daily and intimate contacts with the Olgas and Antonias and Tomases represented God-given gifts. We were serving the "little ones" whom Jesus spoke about when he said: "I have come to bring good news to the poor. . . ." (Luke 4:18). What is more, I took some real consolation regarding our shortcomings from the fact that even Jesus did not always complete the job; even he had not solved all the problems that were presented to him. Early in Mark's

Gospel he rejects his disciples' wish that he go back to Capernaum and finish up the work left over from the day before. "Let us go on to the neighboring towns, so that I may proclaim the message there also; for that is what I came out to do" (Mark 1:37-38).

By the beginning of the 1970s Holy Name Parish had come to what might be called a "double option for the poor." We tried with a fair amount of success to deal with our privileged, upper-class sector out of a clear bias in favor of the victims of their (and our) comfortable status. That is, we looked at life through the lens of the poor and tried to gear every decision with that view clearly in mind. At the same time, we did our best to stay in close contact with the poor themselves—and in this these needy and desperate people provided us with opportunities on a daily basis as they came to us with their many requests for help.

At times we felt as though the "double option" put us in two entirely different worlds when, for example, one of us might return to the parish from the miserable house of a terminally ill Indian man or woman and immediately get a call to the bedside of a terminally ill middle-class Peruvian. The differences between the two deathbed surroundings made us wonder if they existed on the same planet. One evening I listened to a middle-class parent describe the anguish he had felt earlier in the day when his little boy had fallen off a bicycle and suffered a concussion. The man recounted in detail the frantic race to an exclusive clinic in the area, the anxious wait while X-rays were taken and the enormous relief when he learned that his child would come through the ordeal without serious consequences. All of us gathered there with him sympathized with the father's feelings and rejoiced that all came out so well. However, I remembered just a day or two before visiting the shack of a poor family whose three-year-old had swallowed a broken balloon he was playing with and choked to death before anyone could get him help. Two worlds—side by side.

Still, our options remained clear: pastoral attention to all who needed it—and all of it done from the side of and through the eyes of the poor.

CHAPTER 7

The Parishioners React

Despite a high degree of satisfaction with the pastoral attention we continued to give at Most Holy Name, it's easy to understand that the clear shifts in outlook and practice taking place in these years at Most Holy Name provoked reactions of all sorts from the privileged classes there. While a few of these reactions were positive and, indeed, inspiring, I have to say that most proved negative and even antagonistic. During those years I often categorized Most Holy Name Parish as "a battlefield." Privilege hates to be challenged. Nevertheless, despite the conflicts, misunderstandings and outright hostility we encountered among our people, there was never any thought or suggestion on my part or that of my associates of turning back to the "good old days" of parish unity and popularity. For all of us the Medellín analysis and call had been too compelling for anything less than the prophetic posture which the church took at every level of its life, perhaps especially at the level of an upper-middle-class parish like Most Holy Name. We were spoiled for good; new wine had been poured into new wineskins!

A Parish Divided

So it was that our consistent preaching on the social dimensions of God's Word and its call for social change and the modeling of such change through initiatives like the integration of the parish school, together with a questioning and critique of privileged lifestyles, inevitably produced intense reactions. Between 1968 and 1971 I guessed that fully 80% of the core members from the honeymoon years left the parish in one way or another. I have no hard data to back this figure—it's just an educated guess on my part, based particularly on my observations of those first, now mostly disenchanted parishioners. So many of the ones who had welcomed me and celebrated our new church life now turned away. It seemed that droves of parishioners distanced themselves from the parish, some by voicing constant criticism and disagreement, others by actually moving to different parishes—or simply dropping out of parish life.

Most of the dissidents remained nominal members of Most Holy Name but fought the changes at every step and in effect no longer considered themselves active parishioners. Others left quietly, drifting to parishes which had not adopted the Medellín vision—and there were many such parishes, especially in the so-called "residential areas" of the archdiocese where most of the upper classes lived. A few of these parishioners made their feelings known as they left, sometimes quite vocally. One of the original members of Most Holy Name, someone I considered a friend and who had contributed significantly to its early successes, sadly explained to me his reasons for going elsewhere: "You've broken the sound barrier, José. I don't understand religion and church and spirituality in the social contexts where you now locate them. For me, faith is a personal matter between God and myself, having to do with my eternal salvation."

This dissenter had put his finger precisely on the heart of the question, of course, and his complaint was understandable. For generations in Latin America, as in so many other areas of the world, Catholic teaching and practice had concerned themselves with the spiritual life of the individual to the exclusion of any corresponding concern about the social injustices of that continent. Now the church found itself playing catch-up with many of its members who had learned only too well this intensely personalistic view of spirituality. At the same time the Latin American church was forging pathways into deeper and broader understandings of the Christian's life in God. Vatican II and Medellín, to name just two sources of these ideas, were saying that the believing person would come to a better relationship with God to the extent that he or she engaged with a hurting world. The amazing statement from the Catholic Bishops' Synod of 1971 underscored this twofold task of the church: "action on be-half of justice and participation in the transformation of the world fully appear to us as constitutive [essential] to the preaching of the gospel" (Medellín Document No. 6: "Justice in the World"). In other words, for the person of faith this new call to remake an unjust world was itself a way of knowing God and living the gospel more authen-tically. Nowhere was this two-pronged pastoral task more at work than at Most Holy Name Parish, but many of our people either didn't get it or rejected it.

Other parishioners complained that the North American religious of the parish—and I, in particular—had somehow come to dislike (some even said hate) them and their "middle-classness." In part this opinion surely came from the initial, perhaps overly aggressive way in which we brought on the message of Medellín. As mentioned previ-ously, it was as if we North Americans and the parish council had wanted to make up for lost time in the parish and the understandable response on the part of the parishioners to our passion and enthusi-asm was defensiveness and hurt.

In point of fact, nothing could have been farther from the truth in our minds. We knew ourselves to be middle-class, part of the privi-leged minority, part of the problem for the oppressed classes in Peru, and indeed for the entire world. In fact, when a few of the expatriate missioners attempted to turn away from their middle-class roots our reaction went in exactly the opposite direction. I remember visiting the squalid shack of an Australian priest in a slum area of Lima and listening to his views about "becoming truly one with the people." He had taken a job as a taxi driver and lived alone in the most dehu-manizing conditions. While I felt some admiration of his passion for being in solidarity with the poorest people there, and even felt some guilt about my own comfortable living situation in comparison with his, I knew that I could never live like him. Some months later I wasn't totally surprised to hear that the poor fellow had suffered a breakdown and returned to Australia. We reaffirmed the fact that we would never be anything else but white, American middle-class men and women. We knew that the message of Medellín, while directed toward Latin America, applied just as much or more to us in North America.

In addition, as mentioned in the previous chapter, we continued to minister zealously to all members of Most Holy Name as we had always done—visiting their homes, attending to their sick and dying, constantly celebrating the sacraments. What was new about our relationships with these middle-class peers of ours was two things: we increasingly saw our responsibilities to them as including the social context of injustice that existed all around us; and we were quickly expanding our pastoral concerns in order to deal seriously with the domestic workers and the caretakers (initiatives which will receive greater attention in the following chapter). Far from hating our middle-class parishioners, we considered ourselves very much part of them.

No Longer Popular

These criticisms leveled against me and the other Franciscans, together with the departure of so many parishioners, proved immensely difficult for us North Americans. Much of our pastoral training in the United States had stressed the unifying role which gospel ministers are supposed to play. Unfortunately, we had heard very little of the harder sides, the prophetic dimensions, of ministry in that training. We had come to Peru in hopes of building up a weakened church, spurred by its calls for help backed up by directives from the Vatican. Personally and culturally, too, as North Americans it was important for us to be popular and well liked. In the early years when we heard people call us "*muy simpáticos*" (very likeable) it was music to our ears. Now we found ourselves dividing people, provoking conflict, even driving people away from the parish we had so successfully begun. We were most uncomfortable with this divisive role we found ourselves playing.

I often found myself examining my conscience over this unexpected and really unwanted position as party spoiler, scrooge, curmudgeon. Had I missed something? Was there a better, gentler way to challenge our parish and societal status quo? Should I resign as the chief irritant in the parish? But these frequent examinations of conscience never failed to bring me back to the conviction that this unpleasant course was the correct one. After all, the shift in pastoral emphasis from our consoling, even pacifying approach at Most Holy Name, an emphasis aimed chiefly at the privileged class, to this more challenging, even disruptive role had come directly from the great conversion moment of the Latin American church at Medellín. It had not been my idea; I could never have thought it up. Further, the Medellín Conference itself had resulted from that historic, Spirit-led event, the Second Vatican Council, which itself came from Good Pope John's inspiration that the whole church needed to "read the signs of the times" of the twentieth century. In our minds there was no other place for us and Most Holy Name Parish to go—no way back to the innocent and ultimately misdirected years of unexamined ministry in that parish. The only pathway, I concluded, was forward. This conclusion did not make the road any easier in practice, however,

Finally, our soul-searching about the conflictive and divided community which Most Holy Name Parish had become led us beyond Medellín and Vatican II and Pope John XXIII to reflections on the gospel and Jesus' own example. We recalled again and again that the Master had indeed shown himself open and amenable to all with whom he had contact. He was cordial and concerned even with regard to individuals of the very class he so criticized—the pharisees, the scribes and doctors of the law. For example, he ate at the home of Simon the Pharisee, patiently answered all their religious questions on numerous occasions, even allowed one of them, Nicodemus, to come to him at night when the man was afraid to approach Jesus in the daytime. However, one can hardly find more scathing words in Scripture than the Lord's description and condemnation of this oppressing class of his day. "Woe to you Pharisees . . . you frauds . . . blind guides . . . whitewashed tombs. . . ." (Matt. 23:13-39). During those years of drastic changes at Most Holy Name we often reflected that the human reasons for Jesus' death could be traced directly to his increasing challenge to the power structure of his world. "If we let him go on like this," said the chief priests and the pharisees, "everyone will believe in him, and the Romans will come and destroy both our holy place and our nation." And the chief priest responded: "You do not understand that it is better for you to have one man die for the people than to have the whole nation destroyed" (John 11:48-50). It is important to note that while we never went so far as to equate our right to criticize the status quo with that of Jesus' (people like Gustavo Gutiérrez always kept us aware that our social analysis was an inexact science and open to many interpretations), we did take comfort and encouragement in the knowledge that the Lord's own ministry seemed to be characterized by increasing conflict.

A telling conversation between the cardinal and me one evening helped me put some of these conflicts and divisions into context. I had asked for an appointment with the cardinal to talk with him on an administrative matter and when that issue was resolved, the cardinal took the opportunity to ask me why so many critical letters about Most Holy Name Parish were appearing on his desk. Without a moment's hesitation, and quite in earnest, I answered that those letters and the conflicts in the parish were the direct result of the Medellín documents which, I said, he had helped craft and had signed. Upper-middle-class people, I told him, did not take kindly to what Medellín had proclaimed. It was clear from his response that despite his decisive role at Medellín, the cardinal instinctively shied away from the confrontations and divisions which the implementation of that Conference was producing among privileged people in his archdiocese. Incredibly, he suggested to me that the Medellín documents might better wait for another generation before being so openly proclaimed. In my surprise I could only reply that now is all we have and now is when we must preach justice. To his credit there was absolutely no suggestion on the cardinal's part that because of our differences and the letters he kept receiving from our disgruntled parishioners I might be removed. We simply stood up and as I asked for his blessing, he said, "Let us both continue working for the good of the church, José." Nevertheless, I couldn't help thinking as I drove home that his idea of what was good for the church seemed much different from mine—not a comfortable realization.

Positive Responses

To be sure, there were parishioners who both understood and, however painfully, accepted the new pastoral approach at Most Holy Name.

A lawyer for an international bank who had formed part of the parish council remained active in the parochial community. One Sunday after Mass I asked him why he continued to stay at Most Holy Name when so many of his peers found life more comfortable elsewhere. The lawyer admitted that our homilies spoiled his Sunday morning breakfast most weeks but he felt compelled to stay in the parish and have to consider the social changes which challenged his self-interest, "so that I can look at myself in the mirror each morning." I was reminded of Jesus' words to the Scribe, "You are not far from the reign of God" (Mark 12:34).

At a civic meeting one evening another parishioner, an engineer, made an intervention which I judged to be a direct result of what he had been hearing at Most Holy Name. It surely came with no prompting from me. In response to some predictable complaints from several well-to-do homeowners about the poorly maintained parks, dusty streets and bad-tasting water in their subdivision, my engineer friend spoke up and said that these were not the real problems of their neighborhood. What should concern all of them, he said, was the insult to the poor who lived in the vicinity which their own quite comfortable homes and pampered lifestyles represented.

Others who really believed in the Medellín vision and heard it constantly articulated in their parish made serious efforts to implement it in their professional lives. Another engineer, a friend of mine who had successfully constructed high-rise buildings in earthquake-prone Peru, turned his attention to the precarious adobe (hardened mud) dwellings of the poor. These homes were a step up from the straw walls and dirt floors of the caretakers but they were still substandard and very dangerous to be inside when a strong tremor happened, which was often. My friend set out to design low cost adobe houses in such a way that they would survive the swaying and cracking when the ground under them shifted. Another frequent visitor at Mass in Most Holy Name, a law professor at the Catholic university, came to the conclusion that the "justice" system in Peru was basically unjust. Only those who could pay for legal help got it. (Couldn't the same be said of U.S. justice?) He began to educate his students to the moral obligation of taking low-paying or pro bono work, and getting them to consider placing their skills at the service of poor people who were shut out of any legal assistance. A doctor, trained for open-heart surgery in the United States, refused offers to return to the First World and practice sophisticated medicine for older people there. He said that, even though it meant sacrificing his own career advancement, he felt he had to stay and "perform commonplace operations like appendectomies so that younger people in Peru might have a life." "Peru has given me a great deal—I cannot fail to pay it back." The C.E.O. of a publicity agency utilized Peru's rich Indigenous language and customs in his advertising, thus providing a public valuing of the culture of the poorest and most undervalued sector of Peruvian society.

Above all, it was the members of the parish council who best articulated the consequences of what the church had called for at the Medellín Conference. The council members continually taught me and my North Americans colleagues the concrete and often very "secular" applications of that Conference to life in Peru. One evening at a parish council meeting the surgeon mentioned in the previous paragraph explained to us Franciscans his view of what our appropriate role should be in the parish. We were not, he said, to be the leaders or directors of movements for social change; much less should we see ourselves as agitators for particular reforms. Ours, the doctor told us, had to be pastoral care for the laity who carried the Medellín vision into the secular world day after day. We needed to encourage, challenge, console, listen to and pray with and for the lay women and men of faith, who were seeking to build the reign of God in their 9 to 5, Monday through Friday realities. For me, in particular, that lesson was one of the final building blocks in the construction of the new Most Holy Name Parish. The doctor's vision completely turned over in my mind not only the clergy's place in relation to the laity. It also reversed the image of the parish from a safe, somewhat otherworldly religious enclave to a center and resource for vigorous and ultimately risky secular activity. Most Holy Name became a place of "moral discourse," where on formal and informal levels the great questions of that day and that place were debated and courses of action decided. I never forgot his insight, and it has made total sense out of my work as a priest and pastor ever since.

A few months after the doctor's impromptu lecture to us, two members of the parish council followed through on this vision of respective clergy-laity roles in quite a dramatic way. The cardinal of Lima had spoken at the Second Vatican Council in favor of reintroducing the permanent lay diaconate. Now, in these post-Council times he naturally wanted to show the way and establish this form of ministry in his archdiocese. In a classically hierarchical approach, the cardinal instructed all of us pastors to send two or three laymen from our respective parishes to a meeting where he would invite them to courses of preparation to become deacons. I called in a couple of our more outspoken parish council members and asked them to attend a meeting, without advising them of the reason for its being called. I wanted them to respond to the cardinal on the spot as they saw fit.

On their return that evening the two men reported that after listening to the cardinal outline his plan, they respectfully dissented, explaining that in coming to understand and respond to the enormous demands on them as laypeople of faith in the underdeveloped world of Peru, there remained very little time in their lives for such "churchy" ministries as the diaconate. This was not literally true because both of these laymen were dedicated and active members of the parish council—involved, therefore, in the church. Still, as they told the cardinal, they didn't feel any attraction to joining the ranks of the clergy. They had quite enough on their plates as laymen. After their vigorous and well-articulated vision of the lay vocation, they told me, the cardinal decided to postpone for the time being any plans for the lay diaconate.

A Parish Council Initiative

Around this time, some five or six years into the life of Most Holy Name, the parish council took a dramatic step with regard to financial support on the part of the parishioners. The principal means which the parish council eventually chose to support Most Holy Name was one which showed enormous creativity: a complete overhaul of the system for collecting ordinary parish contributions. From the beginning at Most Holy Name I expected that the Sunday Mass collections would serve as the principal source of support in the parish. In addition stipends collected for Mass intentions, baptisms and weddings would augment the income—all of this in the U.S. style of members' support for their parish. The problem was that the system never worked at Most Holy Name; it increasingly failed to cover the administrative and pastoral expenses of the parish. And now, after over four years, the parish was expected to be self-supporting, with few if any subsidies from the New York Franciscan province.

The parish council discussed the situation at length and decided that the system of collections in church and stipends for the sacraments did not suit the Peruvian mentality. We like to keep our religious ceremonies separate from money considerations, went the argument. It was a cultural thing. The council, therefore, proposed a stop to all collections at Mass and all "offerings" for the celebration of the other sacraments, in favor of a system of direct support, a sort of tithing, of the parish by its members. After unanimous agreement in favor of trying the new approach, members of the parish council preached the homily at all the Masses two Sundays in a row and presented to the parishioners the rationale and procedures for the new system of direct support in Most Holy Name.

Their argument, as they worked it out and presented it, appealed to common business sense—the beneficiaries of parish services should support them and those who provided them. It appealed as well to the pride which the parishioners felt for their parish and the attention they were receiving. Should the new approach fail, said the council members, the Franciscans would seek paid teaching positions as religion teachers in the many private and public schools which would welcome their services. This, the homilists explained, would mean of course that pastoral attention in the parish would be severely reduced.

The council's proposal for direct parish support was received with enthusiasm by the majority in Most Holy Name and direct contributions to the parish from then on did cover our expenses—the physical plant and parish salaries, as well as the many urgent appeals for charity from poorer sectors of Most Holy Name. Thenceforth we celebrated all Masses for the spiritual and temporal welfare of the parishioners. People who wished a "special" Mass for a deceased loved one or for a particular need wrote that intention in a book placed at the entrance to the auditorium. All sacraments were celebrated without any mention of the "stole fee" or "stipend," an approach which, by the way, encouraged poor people in the parish to receive the sacraments and which indirectly helped along what would soon become equal pastoral attention to all of the parish's social levels. The domestic workers and the poor caretakers had equal access to baptism and matrimony, for example, since none had to come up with the euphemistic "offering" for the sacramental service.

Under this new system, which was implemented immediately, it happened that sometimes direct appeals had to be made for special parochial needs. For example, a severe seismic tremor shook the parish auditorium during Mass one Sunday morning. I had often wondered how I would react in such a situation. Tremors and earthquakes truly terrified me. On this occasion I was in the middle of my homily when the tremor began and started to build in intensity. Fortunately (providentially) I managed to hold down my panic and directed the congregation to walk to the exits. By the time we got outside the shaking had stopped. Back inside we finished that Mass in record time. That particular shake left the rear wall considerably weakened. Extra funds were needed to reinforce the wall and prevent further deterioration of the building. The following Sunday I simply explained the situation and asked people to place an offering for the repair of the building in collection baskets at each of the entrances. At the close of the Masses that day the parish had enough for the necessary construction work. This exception to the rule of direct support on the part of parishioners served to underscore the effectiveness of the system which the parish council created. Clearly it had become the driving force at Most Holy Name Parish.

Discussion Groups

As a way of discussing in depth what was going on in our parish and the new *línea* (pastoral orientation) of Most Holy Name, I decided around this time to initiate group discussions in the parishioners' homes. The other Franciscans and I, with the blessing and assistance of the parish council, created a series of topics related to the Medellín documents and a process for reflection in small group meetings to be held in various households of the parish. The objective was at once to explain the parish *línea* and to help people conscientize themselves to the social implications of the gospel, a kind of complementary effort to what was going on all around the parish.

During the rest of my years at Most Holy Name these "Conversations about Christian Orientation," as we called them (the acronym in Spanish, CHOC, was much more expressive), functioned with considerable success. We designated what we thought were affinity groups of parishioners and asked for a six-week commitment to the process. One night each week, meetings would take place in the home of a group member and either one of us Franciscans, or more commonly a lay member of the team trained to lead the discussion, would guide the group of five or six couples in what was actually a replication of the Medellín process: social analysis and theological reflection.

Given the dissention which swirled around Most Holy Name during those years, it is interesting that the "Conversations" worked as well as they did. While we did not avoid any of the more conflictive subjects of social injustice and change, including those always threatening lifestyle questions, all of the groups completed their six weeks with the participants seeming to come away with a grasp of what was happening in their church and parish. Perhaps our success was due to the natural graciousness of middle-class Peruvians who never want to *quedar mal* (look bad), in this case by dropping out of a process to which they had committed themselves; perhaps it was the relatively brief time of the "Conversations" or the fact that they took place in each other's homes. It might have been, too, that the novelty of a "home Mass" at the end of the sixth session held the groups together. Whatever the reason, I considered this initiative one of our most successful in terms of explaining Most Holy Name's *línea* to the parishioners.

The "Conversations" achieved a two-fold purpose. In addition to helping people understand what was happening in their parish as a result of the wide-ranging changes of the Second Vatican Council and, especially, the Medellín Conference, the gatherings enabled us Franciscans to keep up with the growing numbers of families moving into Most Holy Name. In their own way the "Conversations" were analogous to the Christian Base Communities which had begun to proliferate throughout Latin America.

Paying the Price

Despite these positive responses to the new vision being implemented in Most Holy Name, exemplified by such initiatives as the "Conversations" groups or the individual examples of parishioners who understood and implemented the Medellín vision, we had come to be and would remain a parish divided for the rest of my years there. My most vivid memory of those years as we moved from a principally consoling to a challenging ministry is that of constant, almost daily conflict. I remember being in New York for some business with my Franciscan province there and waking up in the morning to the usual feeling of tension at facing another day. It was only after a few seconds that I realized where I was, far from the conflicts of Most Holy Name. The experience made me aware of the toll which our ministry was inevitably taking on all of us there.

In another way this awareness of the cost to all of us was heightened when new pastoral personnel would be sent from my Franciscan community in the United States We were in need of their services at this time, since a few of the Franciscans who were with me almost from the beginning had left Lima for various reasons not related to our work there. The newcomers invariably found themselves unprepared for the situation at Most Holy Name—assigned to a parish in a foreign country, the likes of which none of them had ever before experienced—a consoling and challenging place and one that was divided yet dynamic. It was a new experience for those who came and, unfortunately for us who remained, most of them failed to grasp what was happening and returned to the United States.

One of these well-intentioned but unprepared (for the Latin American church of that time) Franciscans lasted just a year and, as he took his leave of us to go back to the United States, told me that he simply lacked the background for what we were doing at Most Holy Name. Another Franciscan who came to help out got engaged in a conversation with an affluent couple one evening around the subject of the Peruvian government's restrictions on the possession of foreign currency. Without any preparation for the topic, or indeed for any similar issue, the newcomer agreed with the couple that it was an injustice on the part of the leadership in Peru to take away their "hard-earned" dollars and replace them with Peruvian bills. I overheard the conversation and on the way back to our residence pointed out to my brother priest the rationale for the government's action. He understood it at once and realized how unprepared he was for the unique situation in which he found himself. His stay with us was short.

(I have been asked if my endorsement of the Peruvian government's restriction on private possession of foreign currency somehow contradicted my earlier skirting of the 10% surcharge on monies coming into Peru, described in chapter 3. Quite honestly I never made the connection at the time but in hindsight I would argue that the cases were different. Foreign currencies held by Peruvians represented a loss to the government there, as much of that money eventually wound up in private bank accounts outside that country. On the other hand, we were bringing fairly substantial monies into the country and the goods and services which those dollars purchased would remain there indefinitely. In my opinion, the surcharge on our incoming checks represented a double taxation on us.)

Without newcomers receiving adequate advance preparation for their new assignment from people who understood what was happening in the Latin American church, it was unfair to expect that the newcomers would fit into a situation such as Most Holy Name. We should have insisted that all candidates for ministry at Most Holy Name had to go first to one of the several centers in Latin America where they could learn about the post-Vatican II and post-Medellín vision. I failed in this regard, presuming that those who joined us would somehow catch on.

Despite these "failures" to incorporate new personnel into our ministry, I believe that all of us who worked at Most Holy Name in those years, who had "grown up" with the changes that enveloped the parish, had a sense of purpose, of constructing something worthwhile, of building a portion of the church which, for all its divisions—maybe because of them—was relevant to the realities in which it was situated. For me these were the most productive years of my life.

And so, as the 1970s unfolded, this life-changing experience took an ever deeper hold on me and on the Franciscans and sisters who had walked this pathway from the beginning and understood its internal logic. While the toll on us was high, I believe that all felt good about what we had helped create—a prophetic as well as pastoral parochial life. In a way, we North American religious became a metaphor for that entire parish enterprise—stretched to the limit of our own resilience, yet strong enough not to break apart. Despite all the conflicts described in this chapter, we, and Most Holy Name, not only survived but also flourished in ways we could never have imagined five years before.

CHAPTER 8

Opposition from the Left
and from the Right

I fully expected the opposition which the middle-class parishioners threw at us throughout these years. They felt betrayed, attacked
and ultimately abandoned by what had begun as a wonderful parish
which catered to them in its beginning years. The lifestyle and structural changes which we tried to live and which we preached made
them—understandably, to my mind—defensive and resentful. All of
us North American religious and the members of the parish council
did our best to keep up an open dialogue with our parishioners. But
their anger never surprised me.

ONIS

What did take me off guard, however, was opposition from a totally unexpected quarter—the priests who had invited me to join them
and their progressive organization, ONIS, as the Medellín moment
in the Latin American church was dawning. A few years into my
relationship with these good men, they became a real and surprising
source of difficulty for me. Over the years, all of us who belonged to
this gathering of priests had been deepening our personal and ministerial option for the masses of people who had no standing in Peruvian society—those "non-human beings" described by Father Gustavo
Gutiérrez. The weekly meetings with him, together with retreat-like
gatherings of the entire group each year, provided venues where we
could share the experiences of our people's struggles and encourage

each other in accompanying and supporting their liberation efforts. This priests' movement during those years stood as a source of inspiration for a large segment of the Peruvian church, including, perhaps especially, the large numbers of foreign clergy and religious like my-self who were working there (fully 65% of all the priests in Peru at that time came from outside the country).

Years later, a student of recent Latin American church history told me that Gustavo Gutiérrez had set himself the task of educating the large influx of foreign clergy to Latin American social problems. In this he had great success, at least with those who opened themselves to this unique and crucial understanding of gospel ministry. Gutiérrez never wavered in his insistence that his and our ongoing analysis of the social realities of Peru and Latin America was a function of our vocation as pastors. On one occasion, for example, he took two foreign priests on a three-day retreat for the sole purpose of correcting their increasing tendency to social activism in place of parochial work.

However, the location of Most Holy Name in a comfortable suburb among the privileged classes which made up a significant part of the parish began to give rise to serious questioning among the leaders of ONIS. There seemed to be a growing consensus among them that the only authentic ministries were those that directly served the poor. Around this time one of these priests gave a lengthy conference to lay and religious representatives from middle-class parishes in which he categorically stated that it was impossible to preach the gospel "with a glass of whiskey in one's hand"—an obvious reference to the ostentatious lifestyle of Lima's privileged classes and to us who worked with them.

But it was Gustavo Gutiérrez, himself, who most seriously challenged me and the other priests who worked in affluent parishes. In this as in all of Gutiérrez's thinking the fundamental question hinged on the preferential option for the poor called for by the church at Medellín. He insisted that this option extended beyond personal choices to the institutions of the church. In the case of church parishes, Gutiérrez's thesis went something like this: the church should physically remove itself from geographical areas of comfort and privilege; if well-to-do Catholics wish pastoral attention they should go to the parishes of the poor. More directly, he would say that if the wealthy are really seeking Jesus, the best place to find him is among the marginalized, the impoverished, the "least of the brothers and sisters."

For the North American reader it is important to understand the position which Gustavo Gutiérrez held in the Peruvian church at that time. We are so accustomed to the unquestioned institutional presence of the church among the wealthy and privileged that this challenge which Gutiérrez laid before us could seem a crackpot idea. Nothing could have been further from the truth. Gustavo was the best of all teachers, who backed what he said not only with topnotch theological reasoning, but also with his own personal commitment. There was not the slightest doubt about his dedication to the liberation of the poor, a vision which consistently marked his theology. And despite his growing prominence both nationally and internationally, he lived a style of life in clear solidarity with the poor. We who came to know Gutiérrez in those years loved him for all that he was and all that he did. His opinions carried immense weight, especially with us foreign clergy, who were a particular object of Gutiérrez's concern. He wanted us to minister effectively in his country and church and he worked long and hard to help us do that. What is more, it made sense that the call voiced at Medellín for a "preferential option for the poor" would extend to the institutional presence of the church, and consequently to parishes like Most Holy Name. Those of us who worked in those affluent areas agreed in principle with the logic of Gutiérrez's insight. So we had to do a good deal of soul-searching on this vital question and its practical consequences for us. What Gutiérrez seemed to be calling for was an abandonment of parishes to which we had been assigned by the local church and, in my case, by my order.

Eventually, I decided that while Gutiérrez's thesis had validity with respect to many of the upper-class parishes where the social teaching of the Latin American church remained a well-kept secret, I would not follow his conclusion about our work at Most Holy Name. There, I felt, we had ample justification for the presence of the institutional church. No one had any doubt about the basic orientation in pastoral practice there. People now joining the parish learned from their peers that if they went to Most Holy Name they would hear about *los indios* and *los cholos* (pejorative phrases used to describe the poor). Indeed, Most Holy Name had become a prime example of what happens when serious pastoral work was carried out in Peru and all of Latin America, of the social clashes provoked by the church's option for the poor. Some of the liberation theologians used terms like "class struggle" to describe these clashes, and their theology began to get criticized in conservative church circles as "warmed-over Marxism," but the other Franciscans and I felt strongly that our ministry in Most Holy Name was very much in line with Medellín and should continue.

To his credit, Father Gutiérrez never called the question. That would not have been the Peruvian way, which avoids direct confrontation if at all possible. Additionally, it is likely that Gutiérrez himself had some practical doubts about pushing this thesis very far. And he had enjoyed good relations with Most Holy Name, beginning with those significant three nights in May of 1968 when he and his colleagues spoke to our parishioners. In any case, the small group of priests in the ONIS group who served in the affluent sectors of the archdiocese settled into what I felt was an uneasy coexistence with Gutiérrez and the rest, and life went on.

Two quite different results emerged from this standoff. First, while I knew I would never forget the education I had received as a member of this priests' group, I never again felt entirely comfortable there. There would always hang over me the memory of a near-ultimatum—get out of Most Holy Name or get out of our group. Second, and paradoxically, several ONIS members, including Gutiérrez himself, occasionally called upon me and the facilities of the parish for help with particularly difficult cases.

In relating this painful experience with Gutiérrez and the ONIS priests, I cannot forget my immense and enduring feelings of gratitude to the Latin American church and to its liberation theologians, chief among them Father Gutiérrez himself. That church and those leaders helped me and many like me come to a deep and lasting conversion to a totally new way of understanding faith and religion. Whatever my differences with individual members of this group, I will always give thanks to God for having allowed me to walk with them. I believe that the other Franciscans and the women religious who served at Most Holy Name during those years feel similarly blessed.

As I recounted in chapter 5, after the brutal 1973 military takeover in Chile Father Gutiérrez called me to ask if a prominent Chilean theologian could stay for a few weeks at Most Holy Name. The man had been placed on a list of "subversives" to be shot on sight, and only immediate high-level intervention from the Chilean Catholic Church made it possible for him to leave the country. He needed a safe and comfortable refuge after that ordeal, and Most Holy Name offered both. I remember the phone conversation with Gutiérrez when he asked this favor: "The man really needs help, José." Thus, Most Holy Name, for all its unacceptability in theory, could provide a haven for one of their colleagues.

On another occasion, an expatriate priest working in a conflictive zone of Lima suffered a temporary but serious case of burnout, and again the priests' group turned to Most Holy Name as a comfortable place where the man could recuperate. It seemed that, despite their misgivings about the appropriateness of a parish in the suburbs, a grudging appreciation for the usefulness of our parish emerged among these progressive priests. I later found out that the ONIS group also secretly admired the pastoral options we had taken at Most Holy Name. Years later, during a chance meeting between Gutiérrez and me at the University of Notre Dame in Indiana, he commented that Most Holy Name in its day had represented an important pastoral option in the wealthy sectors of the Lima Archdiocese. High praise from a man who did not easily give it. I felt that this remark vindicated my decision not to abandon the parish.

Opus Dei

Another source of opposition came from Opus Dei. This quasi-religious order (technically a secular institute, now under Pope John Paul II a non-territorial, worldwide diocese) in the Catholic Church traces its roots and beginnings to the time of anticlericalism in Spain in the latter half of the 1920s. A decade later Opus Dei (Latin for "God's Work") began to flourish under the ultra-rightist Franco regime and in the course of its 70-year history has spread to about 60 countries around the world. In 1953 Opus Dei arrived in Peru. With a membership of devout Catholics drawn almost exclusively from the most influential sectors of society, it boasts a highly centralized, somewhat secretive, and exceptionally disciplined grouping of laity, priests and bishops. During my time in Peru, members there were instructed to keep their affiliation with Opus Dei to themselves, though they could reveal it to their parish priests. The members dedicate themselves to personal sanctity and ethical conduct in daily life, guided closely by priest spiritual directors.

Aside from what seemed like really excessive clerical control in the Opus Dei structures, during the first years of the parish we had no particular difficulties with the organization's members who were parishioners of Most Holy Name. On the contrary, in the days prior to the great awakening of the Latin American church at Medellín, they were among the most exemplary parishioners. Almost all of them attended daily Mass and their private lives reflected the intense spiritual direction they received regularly at the Opus Dei center in Lima. They were strictly Catholic and entirely sure of what was right and wrong, seeming to live in a black and white theological world. On one occasion I asked one of the Opus Dei parishioners, an architect, to speak to a group of young parishioners about his profession. It was to be a straightforward secular talk without any particular religious content. Just an explanation to a group of teenagers of what it meant to be an architect. To my surprise the man answered that he would have to take the matter up with his spiritual director, and to my utter amazement the priest refused permission.

This may be a product of my imagination, but in retrospect it seems to me that the parishioners who belonged to Opus Dei treated me with a sort of benign tolerance, bordering on condescension. Franciscans evidently posed no threat to their view of the world. In those early years I counted a few of the Opus Dei members among my closest friends. Had I been a Jesuit, it might have been a different story, as Opus Dei had historical and ongoing differences with that sophisticated order.

However, as time went on I found that the adherents of Opus Dei never seemed capable of understanding spirituality, gospel living, or indeed Catholicism itself in terms that went beyond issues of one's personal relationship with God and correct individual behavior. The great social teachings of the Catholic Church from the 1960s onward, especially as these played out in the Latin American church, apparently failed to penetrate the consciousness of these essentially good people. Such concepts and theological categories as "institutionalized sin," "preferential option for the poor" and "social change" remained for them questions of personal rather than societal conversion. They remained stuck in a pre-Vatican II, static moral world.

Was this blind spot with regard to what seemed like clear church teaching due to the organization's roots in ultra-rightist Franco's Spain? Or was it because of the personal history and mindset of its conservative and very powerful founder, Father (now Saint) Josemaría Escriva de Balaguer? Or did its insistence on priestly spiritual direction for its lay members and highly centralized governance preclude any breakout into the ambiguous choices and pluralism of opinion, which the church's social teaching pointed to and even promoted? Whatever the cause, theologically and personally we Franciscans and the members of Opus Dei in Most Holy Name began to part company. Because of the social justice option taken by Most Holy Name Parish, the parishioners who belonged to Opus Dei gradually became vocal critics and opponents of what the parish stood for.

As time went on the rift between Opus Dei members of the parish and all of us who ministered there widened. It often took on annoying aspects. On one occasion the widow of a parishioner who had belonged to Opus Dei insisted against the advice of the members of that group who seemed to feel that only a priest of their institute could do the job properly, that I should conduct her husband's funeral. When the Mass ended I left the altar quickly in order to join the procession to the cemetery, only to find that the congregation had remained in the parish auditorium. An Opus Dei priest had slipped in the side door and was conducting his own fairly lengthy ritual of commendation. I would have welcomed this priest as a concelebrant and active participant in the funeral rite, had he asked me. As it was, he gave the impression of a parallel ritual, even of a parallel religious structure, which was exactly what Opus Dei represented in the Archdiocese of Lima during those years. I once asked the cardinal why he did not insist that the priests of that institute attend the mandatory gatherings of pastoral ministers, which were so valuable in clarifying and promoting the Medellín vision of the Latin American church. His Eminence answered with a wry smile and an embarrassed shrug of the shoulders—it seemed that Opus Dei answered only to their own leadership and to more powerful forces than a cardinal in Lima, Peru.

•

It happened that one of our Opus Dei parishioners accepted election to the parish council. When he heard about this, the cardinal (who seemed to have his own problems with the increasingly independent Opus Dei wing of the church in Peru) marveled that of all parishes Most Holy Name would have a member of that group on its council. He questioned me several times about how the man was doing. We didn't have long to wait for the results. After a very short time the man resigned his council position, explaining that the decentralized debate and decision-making process employed by the parish council (approved and encouraged by me, the pastor) ran counter to his convictions and his experience of church. What he meant, of course, was that in the view of Opus Dei only the priest should set the tone for any such parish body and act as its final arbiter.

The increasing rift between the Opus Dei and the parish *líneas* regarding church and religion was, of course, public knowledge. It was also disheartening for me to see good-willed people tearing at the fabric of the coherent pastoral work we were trying to do at Most Holy Name. For me, the contentious attitude of this group of parishioners represented a growing irritant, somewhat different from that of so many among the upper middle class in the parish. The Opus Dei people were, after all, dedicated and practicing Catholics, fervent in their religious observances, and quite visible, indeed edifying, at liturgical celebrations in Most Holy Name. On the surface, therefore, they seemed ideal members of the parish. However, efforts to dialogue with them about the pastoral *línea* at Most Holy Name generally proved futile, even on the several occasions when I felt it necessary to dedicate editorials in the weekly parish bulletin explaining the differences in theology between Opus Dei and the post-Medellín Latin American church. I often felt that speaking out on these subjects was like punching a pillow. The Opus Dei folks seemed to ignore it.

On one occasion, out of a sense of desperation, I challenged the members of Opus Dei to a public debate on theological matters in an effort to spark a needed dialogue. The event took place in the home of a parishioner, an Opus Dei member, one Sunday evening. Contrary to expectations and my own fears (I had wondered if my educated and articulate opponent might simply overwhelm me with eloquent Spanish), the debate turned out to be civil and pretty even on both sides. It concluded with an admission by those present that irreconcilable differences existed between us. My memory of the debate was that it came down to very different views of Christ's incarnation: I suggested that because of God-with-us the here-and-now world has inestimable value; it has to be taken seriously and made more fit for all of Jesus' brothers and sisters, especially the poor and oppressed; the Opus Dei representative saw in the incarnation a call exclusively to individual salvation as life's objective. Two contradictory and irreconcilable worldviews.

Criticisms of the pastoral work in Holy Name Parish from the leftist priests' movement and from the rightist Opus Dei members in a way left all of us there to our own devices in forging this new way of being parish. The isolation proved lonely and discouraging at times. However, just as we had responded to the strong opposition which had come from the upper-middle-class parishioners when the parish first took up Medellín vision, these new challenges once again drove us Franciscans and the parish council back to those same prophetic documents where we always found our center and compass.

With the parish *línea* questioned on all sides, the task was not easy. Still, we always felt we were on solid ground and the work went forward as an ongoing, gospel response to the Medellín analysis of the privileged classes as "primarily concerned with preserving their privileges, which they identify with the 'established order.'" The work went forward, too, as an implementation of Medellín's pastoral Recommendations, one of which stated: ". . . the pastoral efforts of the church should be directed towards orienting these [elite] groups to a commitment on the level of socioeconomic structures leading to their transformation" (Medellín Document No. 7: "Pastoral Concern for the Elites"). In the pastoral work that we did with our middle-class parishioners, these guidelines from the institutional church were all that we were trying to follow—no more, no less.

CHAPTER 9

A Time of Harvest

I don't remember that things ever finally settled down at Most Holy Name. There was no time that I can recall when a majority of the well-off parishioners became entirely comfortable or at least re-signed to our implementation of the Medellín vision. In so many ways the challenging message of that landmark conference continued to irritate many of the upper-class people in the parish. Still, a time of harvest, of positive results—at least in the big picture—did arrive. One of our achievements, the one which I look back on most fondly, was that no one had any doubt about where the parish stood on the crucial and ever-present questions of injustice and discrimination against the poor. As the parish neared the end of its first 10 years and the number of parishioners reached 2000-plus families, Most Holy Name stood as a clear example of what the bishops and theologians at Medellín had called for: the institutional church standing at the side of the poor. To be a member of Most Holy Name was to accept, or at least to endure, a particular way of viewing and judging every-thing: a way based on how things impacted the most needy. Everyone connected with the parish knew that this approach to life was its driving force.

Most Holy Name in Relation to Similar Parishes

Other parishes in the suburban sectors of the Lima Archdiocese could not help but notice this unambiguous option at Most Holy Name. One evening at a gathering of representatives from several of these "residential parishes," as they were called, discussion turned to the best means of implementing the Medellín vision. Should the "preferential option" be taken immediately, almost without preparation; or should the pastoral team try to lead the people with more caution, after careful preparation? Someone from Most Holy Name—I believe it was a member of the parish council—spoke about our experience of the radical and fairly rapid shift from an essentially pacifying pastoral approach to the prophetic stance the parish had come to adopt. Somebody from another parish argued the need to get people ready for such a shift and make it only gradually. Two quite different views. My friend Bishop Schmitz, who was presiding at the session, spoke in favor of the sort of cold shower approach we had used at Most Holy Name as one which in the end would most surely fulfill the Medellín mandate. He seemed to be saying that if we wait until our comfortable people are ready for Medellín, we would never begin the historic task it called for—we shall always be preparing for it.

This clarity of purpose in Most Holy Name was acknowledged and celebrated at another meeting of representatives from all the parishes in the affluent suburbs of Lima. The gathering was called to elect delegates to a forthcoming meeting of the entire Peruvian Bishops' Conference. (This was the kind of inclusiveness we enjoyed in the Peruvian church at that time; the bishops welcomed pastoral workers from all sectors of their jurisdictions to their formal gatherings. We went to their meetings as active participants and not as observers. We spoke from the floor of the assembly and engaged as equals with the bishops in their small group discussions.) When the votes for our sector's representatives were counted, the four slots allotted to residential parishes in the Archdiocese of Lima went to a religious sister, a Franciscan brother, a lay member of the parish council and me—all from Most Holy Name. It surprised me that the participants from the other wealthy suburban parishes elected us to represent them at the forthcoming Episcopal meeting. I would not have believed beforehand that Most Holy Name had that much standing with our peer groups. It was a moment of sheer joy for all of us who worked in the parish, and an affirmation of Most Holy Name itself.

Young Adults

The parish ignited imaginations on another front, as well: among the younger members of Most Holy Name. With the parish now clear about its pastoral options, a delegation of young women and men, mostly university students, approached me to inquire if I would meet with them on a weekly basis so that they could better understand those options. Each Friday evening from then on some twenty or thirty young people would crowd into the dining room of the parish house, initially to question me about how Most Holy Name had evolved, what was the theology that was driving us and what were we ultimately trying to do. Later the sessions became a clearing-house for thoughts, discussions, debates and proposals among these young folks regarding the implementation of their parish's vision as their lives and careers unfolded. In the beginning sessions I did a great deal of the talking, explaining to these attractive and open-minded young folks how the parish had gotten where it was. Later, as they wrestled with the consequences of their parish's option for the poor in their own lives, they asked me to speak less and I did a lot of listening.

Most of these young people were preparing for professional careers. Their assimilation of the Medellín/Most Holy Name preferential option for the poor would demand profound changes in their way of practicing law or medicine or engaging in the business world. They saw that the skills they were acquiring as university or graduate students should be put at the service of the poor in some way. Their courage and idealism in confronting these hard choices was an inspiration for me and my associates, as these young professionals facing really demanding choices exhibited none of the defensiveness or reluctance so typical among their elders in that middle-class world.

In addition, this young group began to seriously consider the opportunities at hand to transmit Jesus' social gospel to younger members of the parish. For them the church's social teaching had great power: it made sense of their lives and their faith. So, on the premise that the young adults of the parish were the ones best suited to relate to still younger members (they told their now 38-year-old pastor that I was too old to make an impact on the kids), the students requested, and got, a special Sunday Mass each week. We celebrated with them in a nearby park where these college-age women and men gathered with younger children and used the Liturgy of the Word to show them the social dimensions of the gospel. It was wonderful to see this kind of "peer evangelization" at work. The older boys and girls really leaned on the high school and primary school children, insisting that they take seriously this "new" way of understanding the Christian faith.

The Option Continues

The old middle-class mindsets, even among the parishioners who stayed with us and tried their best to understand what was going on, did not easily melt away. When one of the old ways of thinking popped up, we held firm to the pastoral choices we had made. Once a group of well-to-do women approached me and, with obvious good will and some excitement, proposed that the parish sponsor a fashion show to raise money for the night school. Of course, these bright and well-connected ladies had researched all the practical aspects of such an event: securing fashion models, doing the necessary publicity and choosing an appropriate place for the show. They had even gone so far as to get the first lady of Peru, the president's wife, to make an appearance at the affair. When they made their proposal to me, they felt it was a done deal.

For me, however, the idea of a fashion show raised warning signals. I felt that it clashed with the philosophy of Most Holy Name. How could we sponsor the flaunting of expensive clothing by professional models for well-to-do women to purchase, when at every street corner of the parish as well as across the city and country you could see people dressed in rags? I gave the organizers a less than enthusiastic response, but promised them that I would consult with the parish council on the matter. (This was not a stall on my part. We had long since come to assume that every decision of this magnitude had to come from the council. Still, being able to delay in giving the women a final answer was handy, as it took away the burden of my having to refuse them on my own.)

Predictably, the council was quick and unanimous in rejecting the notion of a fashion show under the sponsorship of Most Holy Name, however well-intentioned the objectives of such a spectacle. The end does not justify the means, the council members reasoned, adding that it would not be right to insult the poor in order to help them. The council instructed me to take their decision back to the organizers of the show and try to explain why we simply could not hold such an event in the parish. I carried out their instructions, to the chagrin and dismay of the women, who could not understand our missing the chance to help with the night school (while they, of course, reveled in the comfortable lifestyle the fashion show represented). Once again, as so many times before, people felt rejected or insulted by their parish ministers. Some of these women never returned to the parish.

There was an interesting postscript to this episode. Some weeks later I related the incident to Bishop Schmitz, the auxiliary bishop in charge of the suburban parishes. After listening to the story, he remarked that had the parish council decided to allow the fashion show under the auspices of the parish, the archdiocese would have stepped in to veto the event. In Schmitz's view, Most Holy Name's pastoral option coincided with that of the wider church.

Worship Space

During the ten years since Most Holy Name was founded, its worship space on Sunday was the parish auditorium. The building was adequate and got continuous use. On weekdays Eucharist and the other sacraments were celebrated in a spacious chapel attached to the parish house, while the auditorium served for the constant activities connected with the day and night schools. When we built the auditorium we did not think about it as such, but it did fit well with the Medellín view. The Medellín document entitled "Poverty of the Church" had stated: "We wish our houses and style of life to be modest . . . our works and institutions functional, without show or ostentation" (Medellín Document No. 14).

The cardinal, nevertheless, had a different view. On at least one occasion he urged me to build a large church for Most Holy Name, "so that more people can hear the Word of God," he said. While we had lost quite a number of our wealthy parishioners, enough had stayed to make the financing of a new church building entirely possible, as the cardinal knew well.

Again, however, we held on to the clear option taken at Most Holy Name. My answer to His Eminence echoed the one I had given him on the subject of conflict in the parish. As long as we had sick, hungry, poor people around us, the Medellín vision of a preferential option for the poor surely called into question spending money on ostentatious churches. Again, to his credit, the prelate did not force the issue with me, much less threaten my removal if I did not go along with his wishes on the matter of the parish church. The church was not built during my pastorate.

National Projection

Despite the difficulties and awkwardness with the progressive priests' group ONIS headed by Gustavo Gutiérrez, I continued to attend their meetings and occasional retreats. They continued to help and inspire me in deepening my understanding of Medellín's call for conversion based on the signs of the times in Latin America. I stayed with them, too, because they had become a challenging voice in Peruvian church and society. Just about every question of importance which came up in the ecclesial or civil life of the country during those years received careful and public attention from this clerical body, and people came to look for a word from ONIS on the issues of the day. It was good for our ministry at Most Holy Name, therefore, that I continue with the group, given the place so many parishioners of Most Holy Name held in Peruvian society. We Franciscans, guided by the parish council, continued to speak out on the national and international issues which occupied our people and the ONIS group helped us frame them in gospel contexts.

During Holy Week one year, a group of reputed Marxists, who had legally gained control of a national Peruvian television network, turned to our priests' group for help with its Good Friday programming. In those years the Peruvian tradition was that TV and radio had to fill the traditional hours of Jesus' agony and death on the cross—12:00 to 3:00 p.m.—with appropriate religious broadcasting. The Marxists had no idea what sort of programs to use during those hours, so they asked us for help.

At one of our weekly meetings the ONIS group discussed the pros and cons of this fairly demanding offer and decided to take on the challenge of connecting the Good Friday story, particularly Jesus' seven last words on the cross, with current realities. As we reflected on them, it was clear that each of these words recorded in the gospels had a direct application to the social realities surrounding the lives of all members of society, but especially the poor in that Third World country. "I thirst." "Mother behold your son." "Father, why have you abandoned me?" All of these phrases could be translated into the daily struggles, fears and tragedies with which the oppressed and marginalized lived constantly.

Most Holy Name took responsibility for the beginning segment of the program, Jesus' first words during his crucifixion: "Father, forgive them for they know not what they do." Directed by members of the parish council, the TV crews panned several of the broad avenues in the vicinity of the parish, highlighting the many exquisite homes standing alongside the hovels where the caretakers lived on construction sites. Then a member of the parish council and I had an on-camera conversation about the social forces that produced these glaring divisions, forces that locked both the privileged and the underprivileged into this institutionalized sin, resulting in a minority of haves and a majority of have-nots. The conversation, while not completely exonerating the privileged class, did apply Jesus' words of forgiveness "for they know not what they do" to their situation. At the same time, we noted that the gospel calls all of us to move toward overcoming the existing divisions in Peruvian life, especially on such a significant day as Good Friday.

This first segment of the Good Friday programming projected an overwhelmingly powerful message. It was followed by equally relevant portrayals of Jesus' last words as they applied to that contemporary setting: "I thirst"—the barrios where one water spigot serves dozens of families; "Mother behold your son"—the daily anxiety of women whose menfolk could be 'disappeared' at any moment for their political views; "Father, why have you abandoned me?"—the lives of the masses whose only experience is suffering. Afterwards, the Marxist technicians and directors told us how amazed they were at the uncanny relevance of the gospel as they had heard it articulated, perhaps for the first time, in the light of social problems.

Clearly, by now a certain maturity—a harvest time—had come to Most Holy Name. Not that the old conflicts were over: the fashion show experience left little doubt about the continued stresses which our people felt with regard to our pastoral approaches. But as we approached our tenth anniversary as a parish we felt our *línea*, our course, was set and set well. The parish council continued to direct all aspects of parochial life under the guidelines of the Medellín documents. Its yearly retreat for reflection and its monthly meetings centered on continuous reading and analyses of the signs of the times as they presented themselves in contemporary Peruvian and international events. Those reflections were translated into the preaching and other pastoral activities carried on at Most Holy Name. This method prevented any sort of complacency or "business as usual" attitude from creeping into the parish's life. Ideas seemed always fresh, always new. Having the events of the day set the agenda for our pastoral responses kept us on our toes. Indeed, it was this very freshness and newness which gave rise to what I realize now was "the end of the beginning" at Most Holy Name.

CHAPTER 10

The End of the Beginning

We had a fiesta at Most Holy Name to celebrate its tenth anniversary. I remember a feeling of sheer joy that night as the other Franciscans, the sisters and a large number of parishioners all gathered to mark this significant milestone. (Two Franciscans from the United States, close friends of mine, had come to visit, and for me their presence at the fiesta was the frosting on the cake.) I felt that the parish community had survived the serious challenges and conflicts of the past decade. All indicators pointed to a continuation of our prophetic *línea*. Certainly, the parish had become leaner because of its clear option for the poor, but those who remained were there because they chose to walk (more or less enthusiastically) with a truly prophetic faith community. The tenth birthday celebration of Most Holy Name was a night to remember.

But change was in the air. One of the Franciscans who had joined me early on and had shared many of the ups and downs of the first years had recently made a permanent departure for the United States for personal reasons. Another took leave of the parish to go to another of our Franciscan New York province's Latin American missions where he was needed. And I began to wonder myself whether the time for me to move on might be nearing. It wasn't that I had become tired of it all, much less bored. I still got immense enjoyment from the challenges that this unique and varied pastorate presented almost on a daily basis, and felt I could go on happily working at Most Holy Name for the foreseeable future. Still, several factors pointed to a change in this scenario and the approach of a new day.

One of these, ironically, came from the parish council, that remarkable group which had served as our first and most helpful administrative resource and then had become the principal decision-making body for the parish. One evening around this time, as the council discussed the long-term future of Most Holy Name, one member spoke up and declared, without the slightest hint of resentment or disapproval, that as long as I remained as pastor, none of them would mature as Christians. "You are the founder," he said, "and despite all efforts to decentralize authority in the parish, we will always defer to you." It was his personal opinion, of course, and I judged it an overstatement. I knew that these laywomen and men had always exhibited an adult Catholicism in accepting their role as the driving force behind everything Most Holy Name Parish had done. Perhaps I had missed something, but I never had the feeling that the council members waited for me to point out the direction we should go in any given area of parish life. (In fact, as I noted in a previous chapter, the cardinal of Lima had expressed his concern about who had the final say in the parish council at Most Holy Name.)

Nevertheless, the man's assessment made an impression on me, and I thought about it. The parish's founding priest was still around: perhaps this was the moment for me to take leave of the scene for everyone's good (my own included) and test the validity of the unique experiment which Most Holy Name represented. Could a parish with such an operative institutional option for the poor go forward with a pastor who might have a different leadership style from mine? In the end I had to admit to myself the validity of what that parish council member had said, realizing that I would probably have to act on it in some way.

A whole different set of considerations played a large part in spurring thoughts about moving on. Religious and priests of my generation had understood the vocation to overseas mission almost as a lifetime commitment. Traditionally, Catholic missioners went overseas and, barring unforeseen medical or emotional difficulties, remained in their adopted countries pretty much for the rest of their active lives. There are stories of older missionaries, now living in stateside retirement houses of their religious orders, who even today introduce themselves simply by saying their name and the country where they spent 30, 40, 60 years. "I'm Father Bob Smith—35 years in Philippines." "I'm Sister Ellen Jones—40 years in Brazil." By the 1970s, however, this view of the missionary was changing. Gradually we began to think of ourselves in another and equally compelling way —as people who might well be called to return and do what was being called "reverse mission" in our own country and culture.

During a visit to Argentina in 1973, where I had the wonderful opportunity to serve as a Catholic observer at the first exposure of U.S. Protestant missioners to liberation theology, I had a conversation with a Spanish Jesuit on this changing view of mission. He put the matter this way: there are missioners who will always feel the call to go overseas and stay there; but nowadays there are missioners who go overseas for some years and then feel called to return—as missioners to their own countries. And he said that there are also missioners who continually move back and forth between their overseas assignments and their countries of origin. The conversation proved helpful to me as I kept turning the matter over in my mind. Was I being called to one of the latter two possibilities—returning to the United States for good, or moving between the United States and Latin America?

Whatever I finally decided, it was clear to me that this twofold vocation of mission abroad followed by mission at home flowed from the increasingly obvious need for the developed world to hear from its missioners who had served overseas, who had experienced other ways of being church and observed the reality and all the dynamics of the subhuman conditions endured by most people in the underdeveloped world. I felt that in terms of church life, as well, there was a definite need for the comfortable, even complacent, First World faith communities to learn about their more vigorous and challenging counterparts in Third World areas. Who better to push forward this learning process than the missionaries who had ventured forth from the United States, Canada, and Europe? These reasons for the growing shift in understanding the mission vocation made a deep impression on me, and I sensed a strong pull back to my own United States society and church.

Another factor in my thinking was the ONIS priests' group to which I had belonged now for five or six years. Our discussions had constantly returned to the causes for all of the poverties to which the poor in Latin America were subjected. The international factors contributing to this degradation were increasingly apparent to us all—transnational corporations operating at scandalously high profit margins in poor countries, lending institutions setting impossible terms of payments for fragile Third World governments, raw materials shipped from the poor South to the rich North and sold back again as manufactured goods at exorbitant profits, and the enormously powerful United States government which promoted and served as guarantor of an international economic system that generated and fostered the inhuman living conditions for the poor people in this whole putrid system.

Like all of us in ONIS, I saw firsthand dramatic evidence of just such international injustices and their immediate, concrete consequences during those years. For example, Peru's coastal waters contained enormous schools of anchovy fish and a lucrative industry had grown up around this natural wealth. The anchovy catches were hauled into factories along the coast, ground up and made into high-protein fish meal. Doctors in Peru began to experiment with this food and found it very effective in stimulating the growth of brain cells of children who were retarded at birth due to generations of poor nutrition in their families. If they got to the children early enough with the enriched food, they were finding they could actually bring the little ones up to acceptable mental health standards. However—and here was the system at its most vicious—Peru was forced by its increasing debt to export much of that protein-rich fish meal to wealthy countries where as often as not it was used for pet food! "Balance of payments" was the gentle phrase used to cover this robbery.

As if that was not insult enough to Peru and its malnourished children, I learned that one of the leading doctors in these experiments, a member of our parish, had decided to leave his vital work in Peru and accept a position at a prominent U.S. medical center. This was a striking example of "brain drain," the flight of competent professionals from the underdeveloped to the developed world, another international injustice afflicting countries like Peru. (I happened to be at the airport the day that this doctor left Peru. It was all I could do to acknowledge him, angry as I was at this waste of talent and what I considered the betrayal of his country and its weakest people signified by his move to the United States.)

Reflection on these international realities with my colleagues in the Peruvian priests' group convinced me that mission to my own wealthy and privileged United States society could well be a legitimate call from God. As we North Americans often heard in the ONIS sessions, "Our [Peru's] economic and social problems and those of so many underdeveloped countries begin in your world and who better to speak about them and call for action to remedy them than United States citizens like you who have experienced them firsthand."

In all of this discernment there were some powerful personal considerations in the other direction as well. I had by this time lived in Latin America for fifteen of my seventeen years since priestly ordination, during which time I had matured. Much of what I understood about life, faith and religion had become deeply colored by Latin American realities. I loved that culture and the people, and had dear Bolivian and Peruvian friends, as well as those special bonds which inevitably grow among religious who share the rich experience of serving in places like Latin America. I had no difficulty expressing myself in Spanish and had even looked into the possibility of becoming a Peruvian citizen, thinking for a time that I would more than likely stay in that country for many years. On the other hand, the thought of returning permanently to the United States and beginning all over again did not attract me. I wasn't sure I could cope with the sheer affluence and ignorance of how most of the world lived, which I had seen during visits to my country. One dear parishioner at Most Holy Name put it to me in a stark way when she said: "José, if you go back to stay in the United States, you will die a little." For months, therefore, I agonized over what I should do.

In the end it was my Franciscan superiors in New York who galvanized me into taking the course of action I finally chose. As if they had heard the parish council, the ONIS group and my own personal reflections on the future, the leadership of my New York province invited (but did not order) me to consider a return to the United States. They had decided to create a position in the United States to direct the screening, preparation and placement of the still-significant numbers of United States Franciscans assigned overseas (Holy

Name Province at that time had 100 men serving outside the United States—fully 10% of its total membership). They thought I could handle this office.

As a matter of fact I had unwittingly promoted the creation of such an oversight structure. For years I had argued that most of us Franciscans arrived in our mission assignments with hardly any understanding of the culture, language or customs of the people and country we had come to serve. I had questioned the near-total absence of basic accountability to the sending province which I felt should be expected of missioners. It seemed someone in authority had heard my criticisms and when they finally decided to open an office for mission direction had thought of me.

That invitation by my superiors tipped the scales for me. Whatever my misgivings about possibly making a very big mistake by leaving Latin America and going back to the United States, I still had faith in the fact that the Holy Spirit can and does speak to us religious through our superiors—as well as in so many other of the ways I had used to make this decision: prayer, consultation and reflection. When the New York Franciscans invited me to take up this new work, the matter was closed for me. Late in 1974 I told my New York province and the parish council, staff and friends at Most Holy Name that I would leave Peru within the year and return for good to the United States. I had served at Most Holy Name for almost exactly eleven years.

A Final Initiative

With this change of leadership in sight the parish council took a dramatic step. They had known for years that they really had charge of the parish—that while the other Franciscans and I formed an important, even crucial, part of their directorate, in fact the entire council ran the temporal and spiritual affairs of Most Holy Name. So, at one of their meetings shortly after I announced that I would be returning to the United States, the members brought up the possibility of taking on themselves direct responsibility for the administration and spiritual well-being of the parish, without a resident pastor. Their argument was that with the acute shortage of priests in Peru, especially the relatively few progressive priests who could effectively serve a parish like Most Holy Name, wasn't it logical that the council continue its guiding role and invite clergy in as needed for the parish's sacramental ministry?

It was a bold proposal, but one with great merit. The council had in effect run Most Holy Name Parish successfully for more than seven years now and the members had no doubt about their ability to continue in that role. They knew the kind of priests who would—and the kind who would not—do well in the parish. They also knew that the sacramental dimension of life there was not a full-time job. Hence, they would invite clergy accordingly. The question was whether the hierarchy would buy their idea. We drew up a practical proposal and decided to pursue it on a two-track strategy. First, the Franciscan province in New York which had accepted Most Holy Name as its responsibility needed to agree with handing over the parish to Peruvian laity. Second (and more difficult): the church hierarchy in Lima, who were ultimately responsible for quality pastoral attention at Most Holy Name, had to be brought on board with this breakthrough idea.

The North American Franciscan province had no problem accepting the council's idea. Several leaders of the province had visited Most Holy Name over the years and had seen the competence and seriousness with which the parish council directed every facet of parish life there. The Americans had no doubt that the council would continue the good work being accomplished there, especially maintaining the *línea* (the Spanish word had become popular in our province) or thrust of the parish in its overarching option for the poor. In addition, they knew that those post-Vatican II, post-Medellín years were witnessing any number of similar situations of laity-directed Christian Base Communities all across Latin America. Finally, in practical terms, if the parish council took charge officially at Most Holy Name, the New York province would not have to find a replacement for me or the other Franciscans. To my New York province the council's proposal seemed like a capital idea from every point of view.

The first overtures to the local hierarchy in Lima gave hope that the lay leaders of Most Holy Name might actually receive permission to run the temporal and spiritual affairs of their parish. My friend,

German Schmitz, the progressive auxiliary bishop of the archdiocese, agreed with the council's idea. He had observed Most Holy Name from its earliest days and had consistently celebrated and supported all that had happened there. In conversations with me the cardinal had often referred somewhat caustically to Bishop Schmitz as "your friend." It was clear that His Eminence did not entirely share Schmitz's favorable opinion of what was going on at Most Holy Name. As noted, Bishop Schmitz had been appointed the episcopal vicar for the suburban sector of the Lima Archdiocese and was therefore the first member of the hierarchy to be approached about the future of Most Holy Name. His enthusiasm for the idea gave us a great boost of hope.

But it was not to be, however. Due to an administrative slip-up, a letter sent from New York to the cardinal on another matter made mention of the council's initiative, so that he got wind of it, before it could be presented to him comprehensively. He reacted immediately, cutting short any further steps toward implementing this new way of conducting parish life. His argument was that every parish must have a resident pastor, ordained and duly authorized (by the cardinal). In point of fact, this "ideal" did not come near to being a reality in the Lima Archdiocese due to the shortage of priests. Plenty of parishes had no priest, and the cardinal had to know this when he pronounced on Most Holy Name. My guess is that he felt a fair amount of uneasiness over a parish as sophisticated as Most Holy Name which might operate under the direction of independent-thinking lay women and men. Therefore, under the cardinal's unyielding pressure, the council's innovative and promising model of church died a premature death and, in my opinion, a great opportunity was lost. The New York Franciscan province hurried to find a priest to replace me.

Still, this example of creativity and initiative on the part of the parish council spoke volumes about the maturation of lay leadership in the parish and gave an indication of where Most Holy Name could have moved as a new day dawned in its history. The experience, frustrating as it turned out to be for all of us on the council, did point to a further harvest ready to be gleaned in that faith community. It is fascinating to contemplate what could have emerged had the laity been able to take charge.

As a kind of final "what if" postscript: some years later on a visit to Peru I learned from Bishop Schmitz that at least one parish of the archdiocese had been placed officially in the hands of laity. He cited the proposal we had made at Most Holy Name as a principal reason for those permissions being given. He said that the cardinal and other archdiocesan officials had eventually realized that they had missed a golden opportunity in our case.

Leavetaking

In their search for my replacement the New York Franciscans came up with three priests who proposed a "team ministry" at Most Holy Name. Though none had experienced the post-Medellín church, each had served in Latin America previously, so there was no need for intense language study. They arrived in Lima early in November of 1974 to begin the transition period of getting acquainted with parishioners, learning about administrative details and above all getting to know our parish council. True to their convictions, the members of the council drew up a kind of "white paper" outlining the philosophy of the parish and its general mode of operation. It was a concise summary of much that had brought Most Holy Name to where we were at that point: the Medellín response to the Second Vatican Council, liberation theology, the option for the poor, collaboration on the parish council between laity and clergy. I remember a sense of foreboding when I heard one of the newly arrived Franciscans ask if the reference to "shared homily preparation" in the white paper meant that the council intended to dictate to the priests what they should preach. (The story of Holy Name Parish after 1974 lies outside the scope of this book. And as a vitally interested party I would not be the appropriate one to tell it.)

On the evening of December 30th, 1974, the official termination of my work of eleven years took place at a stark little ceremony in our house chapel. I sat there numbly and observed the "installation" of the new pastor by the priest who was replacing me as dean of the several parishes in our residential area. I have a memory of that summer evening getting dark quite early. I remember, also, that one of the three Franciscans who came to replace me—not the one selected as pastor—slipped a note under my bedroom door later that night. In it he expressed his congratulations for what I had done at Most Holy Name. It was a generous and thoughtful gesture on his part, which I very much appreciated.

On the last Sunday in January 1975, almost eleven years to the day after the first parish Mass, I celebrated the Eucharist for the last time in the parish auditorium. Bishop Schmitz preached a cordial and very generous homily about my work at Most Holy Name and a bitter-sweet farewell reception followed in the parish house. My chief memory of that evening was the presence at the Mass and reception of my friend and former parishioner who had told me years before as he left the parish that I had "broken the sound barrier" on him in giving social concerns such an important place in our preaching. He shook my hand warmly and with tears in his eyes wished me well. I've often wondered since if the tears meant some regret on his part that he had missed out on all that Most Holy Name had experienced—or maybe they just meant that he wished the early honeymoon years could have continued.

CHAPTER 11

Lessons Learned

In the years that have passed since my experience as pastor of Most Holy Name I have reflected almost every day on the lessons those eleven years taught me. The names, faces, peak moments, tragic events and comparisons with other ministries in which I have engaged that spark these reflections frequently take me to a single question: would I do it over again? Would I proceed in the same way if given the opportunity to repeat those years? Inevitably, the answer is: yes and no.

In general terms, yes, I would do it again. After all, the move from a parish ministry that consoled, domesticated, and centered on the individual to one that disturbed, challenged and concentrated on the common good was not my doing at all. In a real way, it was out of my hands. The entire Latin American church had clearly called itself to that historic turnaround. For me and the others at Most Holy Name, the choice had always come down to one of obedience—not blind, unexamined obedience, but obedience in the best sense of the word to a mandate on the part of the institutional church to preach the full gospel. This obedience was reinforced by my own conviction that the mandate was absolutely the right one. Historically, the church had been very much part of the problem in Latin America; at Medellín in 1968 it called itself to become part of the solution. I believed we had no choice but to obey.

I would have done it over again, too, because despite all of the conflicts and divisions which our choices provoked among the comfortable and privileged of the parish, I felt confident that Most Holy Name was proceeding correctly in responding to the realities of all of its members, particularly to the poorest among them. We simply could not have gone on catering to the affluent sector of the parish. I don't like to think where the parish would have wound up had we continued in that direction. The pastoral line adopted at Most Holy Name represented the only gospel approach. It seemed to be what Jesus would have done (what he did in fact do) in similar circumstances.

On the level of personal preference and even bias, I believe I would have repeated the experience, given the rather combative Irish temperament I have, which made it less difficult for me to face the opposition which constantly arose. Since the opposition came from those whose self-interest made them push for a return to the sort of pastoral ministry which would domesticate and pacify rather than conscientize and revolutionize the poor, I had very little sympathy for the selfishness which drove that kind of opposition to what we were doing. Quite frankly, I did not mind a good fight over the principles that were at stake there.

For these reasons and others—reasons of the heart which I felt as I experienced in myself a growing personal sympathy for the poor and their plight—the conclusion is that I would do it again in pretty much the same way. Getting to know women like the poor mother who was turned out of the Maternity Hospital while in labor or the caretaker who saw no injustice in the contrast between the shack he lived in and the near-mansion he was protecting—getting to know these people stirred tremendous empathy in me. Quite simply, I came to love them, and I wanted to serve them in any way I could. I would have to have had a heart of stone not to do so.

Yes, I would have done it all over again.

Yet I still have nagging doubts about the way in which Most Holy Name went about the turn from a superficial pastoral engagement to one which analyzed, spoke about and acted on the most serious problems of Peruvian life, and especially about my role as pastor in this process. Had we—had I?—moved too quickly or too aggressively in correcting our initial option for the rich? What truth was there in the criticism that I had come to dislike, even to despise, our middle- and upper-middle-class parishioners? To what degree was the entire experience an extension of my own proactive and, in the eyes of some, dominating personality?

To the extent that any of these questions has validity—and I believe most of them do—there will always remain healthy second thoughts—tentative "*nos*"—about whether the parish should have been guided the way it was. These doubts have been fed over the intervening years by what I am able to perceive regarding the assessment of my Franciscan province in New York on how I operated in Lima. As far as I could ever determine (we male religious are not very good at sharing hard truths with one another), both my superiors in New York and the Franciscans who came to replace me regarded the first four or so honeymoon years at Most Holy Name as a glowing success story; and the last seven years as politicized, confrontational, divisive—which they were—and pretty much as a sorry failure.

Lurking among these doubts regarding my fellow Franciscans' evaluation of my tenure at Most Holy Name is the curious outcome of my return to the United States. As noted in the previous chapter my superiors in New York had provided the decisive motivation for me to make the move by inviting me to begin a mission oversight office which would screen, prepare and to some extent monitor our province's overseas personnel, which at that time numbered around a hundred priests and brothers in Japan, Brazil, Bolivia, Peru, Jamaica and Puerto Rico.

When I arrived in New York early in 1975 to take up this exciting new set of challenges, my superior confronted me with the startling news that one large group of our missioners had unanimously voted against my undertaking these oversight duties. Some vague reasons were given for the opposition: too much involved with liberation theology, too overbearing in his manner, too critical of other pastoral approaches besides his own. With so many missioners against me, the superior said, the new office for mission coordination was no longer open to me. In effect, the principal motive for my return to the United States from Latin America suddenly disappeared.

After getting over the shock of rejection, I wondered how such a reversal could have happened. Perhaps naively, I concluded that it probably represented a continuation of the conflictive and often misunderstood nature of my record at Most Holy Name Parish, compounded by a significant breakdown in communications between the New York Franciscans and our men overseas regarding the nature of the proposed oversight office and what my role in it would actually be. I picked up the pieces of my life and pretty quickly went on to other ministries in the United States. Naturally, from the outset here the life-changing experiences I had lived through at Most Holy Name marked every aspect of the work that followed.

For some of my friends, however, especially among those I had been close to in Lima, there was a more sinister explanation—a conspiracy theory, if you will. They were convinced that the cardinal of Lima, tired of the conflicts at Most Holy Name, persuaded my Franciscan superior in New York to entice me out of Peru with a fictitious job offer. The whole episode remains a curious one and has fed the doubts I feel regarding my accomplishments as pastor in Peru.

On balance, however, I must say that I hold positive memories and a positive opinion of those accomplishments. I recognize that there were many shortcomings in my efforts to make of Most Holy Name a faithful representation of Christ's Body in the Latin American church of that time, but I really don't believe I would have changed a single important initiative we took during those years. That's the "yes" answer to the question about doing it over again. The "no" part revolves around the *way* in which I would have done it.

Charity and Justice

Whatever the final assessment of my role in it all, valuable lessons were learned from the story of Most Holy Name's first decade which in my mind justify this entire narrative. They are lessons which, I believe, are transferable and crucial to our own U.S. church. First among them is the all-important distinction between charity and justice and how it translates into pastoral practice. During the first several years at Most Holy Name practically the entire social concern of us Franciscans and the sisters went to works of charity. Outreach to the middle and upper-middle class, as well as to the domestic workers and to the caretakers on construction sites, had the purpose of extending a kindly helping hand, of alleviating the hurts each of those social classes, above all the poor, suffered. That was charity. What that approach lacked was a sense that surrounding all of our parishioners—the middle class and the poor classes—were social forces holding in place a status quo which was entirely favorable to the upper classes and exceedingly harmful to the rest. That was justice.

This pastoral approach of doing good works for everybody lacked a sense of the justice which must ultimately go along with any act of charity and which asks why this charity is necessary in the first place. Put another way, the charity which we initially focused on in Most Holy Name did not include "[charity's] basic expression—justice" as Pope Paul VI had insisted on the occasion of the 1968 Medellín Conference.[1] For the first few years after the parish began no one asked about the *why* of things as they were. The symptoms of poverty and inequity received some attention, but not their causes. We were just putting band-aids on life-threatening infections, just "fooling around" as that Peruvian priest had made brutally plain to me. We came to learn that both charity and justice are necessary, that one without the other makes gospel ministry fall short. This hard lesson, once learned, changed everything in the parish. I believe that it made our work there more authentic and complete—and much more difficult.

There was a time when some of the more radical elements among church people in Peru put forth a contradictory thesis, namely that all works of charity should be discontinued so that efforts to bring about justice could take priority. In other words, the thesis held that works of charity were actually delaying justice, that the poor would rise up more quickly if they were not given painkillers—free food, or medicine, or hand-me-down clothing. Stop doing charity, went the argument, so that the kettle of unrest could boil over faster. It was a harsh idea, not to say an un-Christian one, and I don't remember anyplace where it was actually done, certainly not at Most Holy Name. Poor people often need charity, immediate help with their most basic needs for food, medicine and shelter, or they quite literally will not survive long enough for the slower and more complicated efforts toward justice to bear fruit.

The distinction between justice and charity was real and, once understood, also made all of our pastoral work at Most Holy Name totally understandable. We did the charity out of a sense of compassion for the desperately poor and a desire to alleviate their pain; we pressed toward justice out of compassion and a desire to eliminate the causes of their pain.

Some years later in the United States I heard all of this put in very simple and concrete terms by the charismatic Archbishop of Recife, Brazil, Dom Hélder Câmara. Speaking at the Eucharistic Congress of 1976 in Philadelphia, the archbishop told the audience about his great desire to greet Mother Teresa and "kiss her hands to acknowledge all her work for the poor of the world. But," he continued, "a much more difficult and much less understood vocation is the one which asks 'why are the Mother Teresas of the world necessary?' " Mother Teresa did charity; Dom Hélder went further and did justice. On another occasion, he spoke from his own experience of how misunderstood the demands of justice can be: "when I feed the poor they call me a saint; when I ask why there are poor, they call me a communist."

The Personal and the Societal in Jesus' Ministry

A corollary to these charity and justice requirements of the gospel, one which we thought about often during the years of change at Most Holy Name, gave us encouragement and a lot of consolation as we moved through those years, and this deepened as time went on. It centered on clear gospel evidence that Jesus showed concern both for individual and societal realities. His care for people like the widow of Naim, the man with the withered hand, the ten lepers, and many others, seemed limitless. People came to him from all sides and he did his best to serve each, so much so that his own family thought he had "gone out of his mind" (Mark 3:21).

At the same time he showed a keen awareness of the social, structural, political framework within which he and everyone else was moving in first-century Palestine. "Render to Caesar what is Caesar's" (Matt. 22) is a political, economic statement, as are many of Jesus' parables, such as that of the Good Samaritan in Luke 10. We have the case of the widow at the temple in Mark 12, who, Jesus points out, contributed "everything she had, her whole sustenance." Some scholars see Jesus' words here as a rebuke to the religious authorities there for exacting so much from the poor. In fact, the Jubilee concept outlined in the Hebrew Scriptures, where God mandated the periodic restoration of right social relationships, runs across virtually every page of the gospel.

We at Most Holy Name thought about this "double vision" of Jesus' own ministry. It became clearer and clearer to us that when the Latin American church turned its pastoral attention to the real problems of that world, it was simply following Jesus' own example. The documents of Medellín dealt with extreme sensitivity even with the elites of Latin America—those people who had so much to answer for—just as Jesus had done in his time; but they also made a strong call for deep changes in the economic and social patterns which favored the elites over the majority poor. This was Jesus' own message and example.

Jesus' Consoling and Challenging Ministry

Flowing directly from our reflections on the personal vis-à-vis the societal dimensions of Jesus' ministry was another crucial lesson. Despite his fairness and concern for each person of the privileged class, Jesus continually challenged them. It became clear to us at Most Holy Name that if we presume to work in the Lord's name (and what else is gospel ministry?) that work must involve both consolation and challenge; it requires both a pastoral and prophetic approach—often with the same people at the same time. This learning lies at the heart of this book and, I believe, has deep implications for all ministry in the First World.

The gospels speak of a comforting message for every person in the crowds that followed Jesus ("Come to me all you who are weary and find life burdensome and I will refresh you . . . ," "My burden is easy, my yoke is light . . . ," "Fear is useless"). He dealt kindly even with individuals of the privileged class—with a pharisee like Nicodemus, for example, who came to him by night, too afraid to appear with Jesus in the daytime, or with Simon in whose home Jesus ate a meal. Yet there are no stronger words in the New Testament than those Jesus directs at that class as the oppressors ("Woe to you Pharisees . . . blind guides . . . frauds . . . vipers' nest! Brood of serpents . . ."). The Lord distinguishes clearly between the individual and his or her social reality, especially with regard to the privileged and powerful in first-century Palestine. We at Most Holy Name came to see that the Latin American church called us to do the same.

However, I never remember that we thought of ourselves as infallible carriers of Jesus' life and work, as any kind of privileged possessors of his truth. Never, to my knowledge, did we say to ourselves that "because they were against us, they must be wrong." In fact, as has been mentioned, we Franciscans and the others involved in the direction of the parish knew our shortcomings and mistakes. We often agonized over the divisiveness which our ministry was causing. But it was a comfort to know that Jesus' own teachings and actions not only met with opposition but on many occasions actually provoked it. This experience was new for us who had been trained as unifiers, friendly with everyone, at odds with no one. We learned slowly that certain topics, such as lifestyle choices and economic injustices, were hot button issues which easily led to conflict. They had in Jesus' time, and they did today.

I often wondered during those years why relatively few of the affluent parishes like Most Holy Name actually took on the Medellín line with all its consequences. In conversations with the pastors of those parishes I would hear a reluctance on their part to rock the boat by speaking forthrightly about the social imbalances which favored their well-to-do parishioners. There was sometimes, also, the argument that "the people were not yet ready" for a more prophetic message. (Tell that one to the poor!) These exchanges with my fellow pastors taught me that we priests more often err on the side of caution and prudence than we do on the side of boldness and confrontation, even in a situations where our church calls us to clarity and forthrightness in our preaching and teaching. I believe, too, that today's bishops fail even more by choosing prudence over prophecy. The problem is not confined to Latin America; I believe that in the United States it is eating away at our soul.

The Ideal of Unity and the Reality of Conflict

Another lesson of those years concerned the question of unity. That sign of Jesus' reign on earth, that which he prayed for at the Last Supper ("that all may be one as you, Father, are in me, and I in you" (John 17:21), had been at the top of the priorities I set for myself and the parish when Most Holy Name began. As a Franciscan I was imbued with an 800-year tradition of bringing people together by mediating and reconciling. For so many people the Franciscan garb has come to mean a kindly, nonjudgmental presence. As the years unfolded, however, it became crystal clear to us that in today's world, at least, unity carries a high price tag and is not easily accomplished. This lesson came home to us painfully as the Medellín vision became an increasing reality in the parish, that is, as we got engaged with the real life of Latin America.

The confrontation one Saturday evening after Mass (see chapter 4), when a member of the parish prominent in political life challenged me about my "Marxist-tainted" homily, highlighted the fact that real unity, and not a superficial papering-over of such essential differences, is a slow and painstaking process. Indeed, I came to wonder if unity can ever be possible in the face of such disparity of opinion. My parishioner and I held completely opposite viewpoints, opposite worldviews. What would it take for us ever to come to agreement?

See from this perspective, Most Holy Name was a divided community in those years despite our increasing clarity of purpose, or rather because of it. The words of Pope Paul VI quoted above could have been paraphrased about us: "a minimum expression of *unity* is justice." Most Holy Name would never enjoy the unity I had hoped for in the beginning because the unjust social divisions among its members, which indeed permeated the entire Peruvian society, remained imbedded there. Our pastoral efforts would always aim toward the day when "all would be one" but all sorts of "isms"—racism and classism especially—needed to be uncovered, overcome and forgiven before that ideal could be realized. Meanwhile, just as in the life of Jesus, conflict was the order of the day and we had to learn to live with it.

One of the ongoing objections to liberation theology has centered precisely on how it interprets these social conflicts. Its critics say that the liberation theologians have appropriated Marx's analysis and promotion of "class struggle." To the extent that the theologians accepted Marx's insight in their analysis of society the critics have a valid, though irrelevant, point. Of course there is "class struggle," as the experience at Most Holy Name amply demonstrated. The powerful pushed down on the poor and to some extent the poor pushed back up. However, to the degree that those opposed to liberation theology see something more sinister in its acceptance of Marx's analysis—fomenting violence, for example, or offering specific formulas for revolution—the critics are wrong.

At the same time, we couldn't let the disunity make us change the direction we had taken. The message of Medellín was clear and unambiguous—opt for the poor. If that produced division, so be it. In fact, it was clear to us that the path to unity had to pass through all of the inequities and injustices present in the Peruvian and Latin American world. You could not quietly sweep them under the rug and call that unity.

Church and Reign of God

One evening I sat in the Cathedral of Lima and listened to a homily by the cardinal. It occurred to me there that His Eminence represented something of what the institutional Catholic Church in Latin America had done when it called itself to break with its privileged past and move to the side of the powerless. Those great architects of the Medellín documents, among them the cardinal himself, had taken an enormous risk, a leap of faith, and put the reign of God ahead of the church's interests. The cardinal's words themselves did not spur this thought—I really do not remember the occasion of the homily or his exact words. What hit me was the breathtaking conversion of the church that he represented and that he had promoted.

In making a choice for the Reign of God over its own security, the church of Latin America at that time again taught that this was exactly the right choice, and Jesus' own priority. Jesus founded the church in the context of proclaiming God's reign. The church was intended to serve the values of that reign—mercy, human dignity, unity, justice, peace and love. The church should never exist for itself alone but only in function of God's "peaceable kingdom."

That evening in the Cathedral of Lima I suddenly understood these things in a way I had not before. It was a lesson which, I now realize, has to inform and support everything any part of the church does. So often this priority of God's reign means a risk for the institutional church and too often we church people—perhaps especially in the First World where we can be hampered by feeling that we have so much to "lose"—shy away from it. But as Medellín showed, there is really no other course for the church. Either we are promoters of the values pointed out by Jesus as signs of his Kingdom breaking in on human history, or we become irrelevant. In a small way, the story of Most Holy Name demonstrated just this lesson. (One visitor from my Franciscan province in New York cuttingly described my ministry in those early years as "inspecting middle-class swimming pools." His assessment a few years later was quite different.)

The Institutional Option for the Poor in Theory and Practice

Without doubt the overriding lesson and the thing that gave greatest satisfaction to us religious and laity, who were intimately involved in the first decade of Most Holy Name Parish, came from the parish's institutional option for the poor. Through this increasingly clear choice on the part of the parish council, the sisters and us Franciscans, the parish became known as a voice for the voiceless in the neighborhood, the city and, indeed, throughout the country. (In a conversation with a sociologist at the Catholic University in Lima about the integration of our parish school I was told that nowhere in Peru or to his knowledge in Latin America was there any similar initiative.) Though we know that when people commented to those moving into the parish. "You're going to hear about the Indigenous and the marginalized," they meant it as a criticism of the pastoral thrust at Most Holy Name, we took these comments as compliments.

This institutional option took many forms, most of them already recounted in this book: our preaching, the challenges underlying all sacramental celebrations, the integration of the school, continued critique of the privileged lifestyle of the middle class (including us religious) in the parish and, ultimately, serious and consistent outreach efforts to the poorer classes. In addition, the poor themselves became more and more aware that Most Holy Name was "their" parish as well as that of the privileged classes. I found this particular outcome of our parish's option enormously heartening. We really had reached the "least of the sisters and brothers."

This perception of Holy Name Parish as a place of refuge for the oppressed and marginalized families in our area came home most clearly during a year when leaders of a group of some 40 poor families living in dreadful physical circumstances at the geographical margin of the parish asked me for a unique favor. They had decided that the location of their houses provided them with entirely unacceptable living space. It was a small, marshy, dank piece of property, filled with roaches and rats, with just one water spigot for their entire population. The children and adults there had a variety of illnesses directly attributable to the subhuman living conditions around them. In the face of this situation, the leaders of the little community wondered if it would be feasible and justifiable for the entire group to move out to a larger, more healthful piece of property a short distance away. The favor they asked me was to sit with them and listen to their discussions, not to give them answers, but to share my thoughts about their idea.

The problem with their proposal was that the area which they hoped to occupy, while entirely vacant, was privately owned. Could they, should they, take the law into their own hands and just go live on the unused piece of property? What would the owner do to them? The government? The police? These were the questions which this little group of parishioners wanted to share with me.

For the better part of a year, I met with this base community, sometimes in the parish auditorium after Mass on Sundays, but most often seated with them outside of the shacks where they lived. I was the listener, the outside presence, and the pastor. I spoke very little at these sessions and only when someone asked my opinion, but they obviously valued my presence, knowing that I was deeply concerned about their living situation.

The outcome of their discernment proved successful, if painful. The small group did occupy the property in question and, after some serious and even violent altercations with the owner of the land and the police, were given another area by the government, one which served them just as well.

What is significant about that experience, in addition to the large victory achieved by some of our poorest parishioners, was their confidence in and reliance on their parish for guidance. They knew we would never betray their trust by warning the authorities of the possible land takeover. They also knew they could count on their parish leaders, myself in this case, to offer advice when they requested it. The whole experience was an example of Most Holy Name's solidarity with those who had no voice, or whose voice had never been listened to. (Indeed, I generally agreed with the moral right this little group had to occupy private but unused property and, after warning them of the dangers involved, let them know my opinion.)

There is a lovely postscript to this story. When the community finally got settled on the new site and began to build their homes there, they called on me again—this time to celebrate the Eucharist with them. "We do not want to live out here [now some miles away from Most Holy Name] like animals," they said. Somehow they connected their successful struggle for more human living conditions with the Bread of Life.

There were daily examples of poor people seeing their parish as a "voice of the voiceless." Often one of us Franciscans or a sister would rush to the maternity hospital in the middle of the night with yet another poor women suffering labor pains. These women knew that they stood a better chance of admission to the hospital at that hour if a priest, brother or sister accompanied them. They knew, too, that the *padres* or the *madres* would not refuse them this service. We made trips to other hospitals and clinics with desperately sick adults and—so often—with dying children, in order to prevent the inevitable response of medical personnel to the poor when they are alone—"there's no room here."

On one occasion I hurried with the sister-nurse and a dying Indian baby to a nearby and very exclusive clinic, only to be told by a doctor on emergency duty that we should take the infant to the children's hospital. In our anxiety over the child's situation, we set out without question for the other hospital, only to have the baby die in the car on the way. When I realized what had happened—that the doctor in the first clinic had not wished to treat a baby because it came from a poor family and was going to die anyway—I returned and confronted him, threatening a law suit. Of course, such a course of action was out of the question in practice, given the poor family's lack of resources and especially given the impossibility of Indigenous folks like these having the time and energy to fight such a battle. Nor would the parish be able to expend its resources on one case; we had similar injustices happening every day. But I wanted to put a scare into those callous medical people, and, judging from what I was told later, I succeeded. They thought the American priest and this unique parish might just have the pizzazz to take them to a public trial.

These daily experiences of attention by the parish to scores of our parishioners (and to others outside the parish) living on the margins of Peruvian society provided continual food for reflection and for the ongoing implementation of our institutional option for the poor. One summer afternoon I found myself standing outside of Lima's only children's hospital with a severely dehydrated, dying baby in the arms of her mother. The line of children ahead of us was so long that we were not able to gain access even to the doorway of the emergency room and the child died there on the hot sidewalk. Passing overhead around that same time were supersonic jet fighter airplanes, twelve of which the Peruvian military had recently bought from France at the cost of $12 million apiece, a $144 million total expenditure. The tableau of a Peruvian child dying because of scarce medical resources while useless expensive military toys flew above us made for deep reflection and challenging homilies back at Most Holy Name. How many children's hospitals, how many emergency rooms, how many nurses and doctors could have been provided with the millions spent on those planes? (The enormous injustice of exorbitant military spending being siphoned off from urgent human needs remained with me as a life-long paradigm for judging similar situations throughout the world. A few years later while working at the Office for International Justice and Peace of the U.S. Catholic Conference of Bishops, I remember helping make this case in a published study of arms sales around the world.)

The sum of these daily encounters with the "least of the sisters and brothers" and their contentment with the parish "on their side" continued to demonstrate that an institutional option for the poor was not only possible but necessary. This remains the overriding lesson learned during the first decade in the life of Most Holy Name. Such an institutional choice to stand with and for the oppressed, the marginalized, the dispossessed goes beyond the preferences of individual priests, sisters or lay folk. It puts the parish, the school, the diocese—in a word, the organized church—squarely on the side of the hungry, thirsty, naked, stranger or imprisoned sister and brother. The Latin American church had called us to that option, and for us it made total sense of the life and ministry at Most Holy Name. I believe it makes total sense of the church's ministry everywhere.

The Cardinal

I have tried to be honest in this book about relations between the cardinal of Lima and Holy Name Parish and myself. They were prickly, at best, for the many reasons and circumstances described in these pages. Still, I left Lima with a sincere appreciation for this man and the significant role he played as the Peruvian church adapted to Second Vatican Council and Medellín.

He had taken part in all four sessions of the council and I felt that he understood the historic breakthrough which Vatican II represented. I've already mentioned that in Peru we did not get tangled up in the kinds of petty disputes over liturgical reforms, for example, which drained so much energy in the U.S. church (Communion in the hand or the Mass in English). When I told the cardinal that I needed lay ministers of the Eucharist to help distribute Communion, his response was, "get them." No fuss, not even a mention of proper preparation— he understood what was important.

His Eminence, of course, knew Father Gustavo Gutiérrez very well as a priest of the Lima Archdiocese. He respected Gutiérrez, met with him privately once or twice each year and understood the value of liberation theology. I believe the cardinal enabled Father Gutiérrez to continue his cutting-edge theological work without the deadening restrictions other liberationists had placed on them by the Vatican. When the priests' group ONIS formed, Gustavo asked for an appointment with the cardinal. He listened as we explained what we had in mind and then told us to go ahead, that we could do the church a great service. (This judgment is remarkable in light of other priests' movements around Latin America at that time which took much more radical positions, in some cases placing themselves outside of the church.)

One of these days a historian will write about the era of Cardinal Landazuri as Archbishop of Lima, which spanned some forty years (he became archbishop at age 38). I have no doubt that the verdict on his long service to that church will prove overwhelmingly positive.

The Power of the Pastor

Perhaps the final lesson learned, as this remarkable experience came to an end for me, has to do with the unfortunate fact that in the Catholic system of parish life the position of the priest remains crucial and definitive. Things can happen or not happen because of this one man. When the Archbishop of Lima refused permission for the parish council to take on itself the spiritual and temporal affairs of Most Holy Name and insisted on a resident pastor there, a new and difficult day dawned. That story is not a part of the present one; suffice to say that practically every dimension of the Medellín vision which had been implemented in Most Holy Name was dismantled with startling speed. Within three months of the new pastorate a member of the parish council flew to the United States hoping to convince the superiors in New York that Franciscans were tearing down what Franciscans had built up at Most Holy Name. He received no hearing. A new pastor was in place and that was that.

We need to find a way through this problem in our church. The Second Vatican Council described us as the People of God, surely a description of equality among us. Yet it seems that some of the people are more equal than others—especially the hierarchy, including pastors. As I reflected on the experience of Most Holy Name, I had to acknowledge that another pastor might not have "allowed" the parish council such scope in decision-making there, or he might have waffled on the implementation of Medellín, or kept the parish school segregated for "prudential" reasons. Too much power resided in me. And the fact that I tried to use it well does not remove the grave problem of overbearing hierarchical structures in a church which Jesus founded by saying, "the greatest among you will be your servant" (Matt. 23:11).

Conclusion

Still, the experience of a parish which under the guidance of the wider church in Peru and Latin America effected its own Medellín moment will remain as the defining time of my life and the lives of others who lived it. I witnessed and engaged actively in a movement, guided by the Holy Spirit, where the much-maligned institutional church at every level revolutionized itself in the best sense of that word. It turned around, converted, took an entirely new path, moved to the side of the poor—and paid a high price for its courage in terms of its former privileged place in Latin American life. The experience has convinced me that you can dedicate your life to such an institution, even when it fails miserably, as so often happens, to live up to that vision in other places. Having known it once, you have to believe that the possibility of other such Spirit-led miracles is always present, even in our faltering and flawed Catholic Church.

The miracles do continue, too. Not long after I left Latin America, a conservative and unpopular (in progressive church circles) bishop was named archbishop of San Salvador. Oscar Romero lasted only three years there before he was shot and killed while offering Mass in a small chapel on March 24, 1980. However, his public and vocal option for the poor of his country—the direct reason for his assassination—stands as yet another work of the Holy Spirit in the institutional church. The possibility of such miracles remains the lasting lesson I took from my eleven years at Most Holy Name Parish.

Notes

[1]The pope said: "Is love enough? Is love sufficient to uplift the world and overcome the innumerable difficulties which oppose the regenerating and transforming development of society . . . ? Are we sure that in the face of the modern myth of temporal efficiency charity is not a pure illusion or an alienation?

"We have to answer: Yes and No.

"Yes, charity is necessary and sufficient as the great propeller of the innovative phenomenon of this imperfect world in which we live. No, charity is not sufficient if it remains purely theoretical and sentimental, and if it is not accompanied by other virtues, *primarily justice which is its basic expression*" [emphasis added] (Paul VI, Address for the Day of Development at Bogotá, Colombia, August 23, 1968).